KU-158-163

STYLE YOUR
MODERN
VINTAGE
HOME

London Borough of Southwark	
D	
SK 2445726 4	
Askews & Holts	08-Jul-2014
747 HOM	£19.99

A GUIDE TO BUYING, RESTORING
AND STYLING FROM THE 1920s TO 1990s

STYLE YOUR
MODERN
VINTAGE
HOME

KATE BEAVIS
Foreword by PALOMA FAITH

Contents

Foreword
by Paloma Faith

I met Kate and her husband, Adam, at a London vintage furniture fair while shopping for my dream mid-century bed. The bed I wanted was from the 1970s with a fabric headboard and built-in speakers… wacky retro and quite rare. I'm drawn to nostalgia and vintage and recently bought my first home; I decorated it all in about 2 months with junk shop finds. It's filled with chintzy glamour.

Even though Kate and Adam didn't have the bed I was looking for it was clear that they were passionate about their vintage business and more importantly, that they understand 20th century design.

Kate has put her passion into writing this book so that everyone else can fall in love with stylish vintage pieces from the last 100 years. Her expert tips and advice for buying, restoring and styling have created something we can not only learn from, but be inspired by, so that we can all style our own modern vintage homes with confidence to create a space that is unique and special.

Paloma Faith x.

Introduction

We live in a modern world with the desire for greater technology and more space, yet our love for vintage seems to be stronger than ever. In a time of fast speed and lack of time we are craving a sense of nostalgia to add contrast to our lives. I have often been asked how to style vintage homewares and furniture without actually recreating a period home, so from this idea *Style Your Modern Vintage Home* was born.

The book covers all decades from the 1920s through to the early 1990s. It provides hints and tips for styling your vintage home in a modern setting with other current pieces, such as your television or computer. You can mix up eras too if you want: many homes feature loved items from different decades as well as modern and antique pieces. Within each era the home has been broken down into key rooms, including the kitchen and living room. Must-have items are suggested, plus cleaning and restoration tips and 'watch outs' to consider when buying vintage, as well as extra finishing touches you may want to consider to complete the look.

Throughout the book there are inspiring photos from real homes filled with great vintage treasures. Many books on decorating homes style amazing spaces that are unobtainable for many of us. Therefore it was important to use real homes lived in by real people that have great style. The homes are also very different from each other and cover all shapes and sizes: Justin and Adelle's home is in the country with beamed ceilings, Sarah B.'s home is a bungalow reminiscent of American ranch houses and Carla and Martin's home is an open-plan city flat. They have kindly shared their thoughts on how they have styled their homes, where to buy vintage and what it is they love most about it.

It is also important to understand some of the social history of the time and how it impacted our homes. Loving and collecting vintage is about being unique, knowing your own style and buying local, but it should also be about respecting the time it came from and knowing as much as possible about its history. So let's love a 1930s enamel bread bin with its slight wear and tear knowing it has survived a world war, or restore a 1960s sideboard, giving it the second chance it deserves when most people discarded them in the 1980s.

Not forgetting that, above all, collecting and styling vintage is fun. The homes featured haven't created this look overnight; they have lovingly added items over the years, re-positioning them each time a new collectable arrives. I hope this book will help you to get the vintage look and also act as a guide for years to come as you create your modern vintage home.

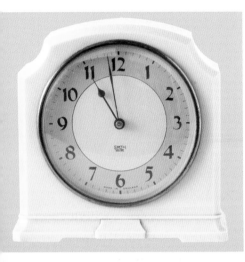

1920s–1930s

The 1920s were a time of hope, with a desire to live for the moment. World War I ended with 16 million deaths worldwide, making it one of the worst wars in history. As a result young people decided to throw caution to the wind and enjoy every second of their lives. They partied, drank cocktails and danced the night away earning their title 'bright, young things'. Even prohibition in America didn't hold them back – driving dance halls and alcohol underground made it even more fashionable to have a good time.

The 1920s and 1930s were highly innovative times, with the invention of the radio in 1920 and the television in 1925, as well as further developments in new materials, such as Bakelite. Commercially, the western world was booming, with couples going to far-flung holiday destinations on trains, cruise liners and airships. They brought back souvenirs from African safaris, such as ivory and tortoiseshell, to adorn their living rooms. The discovery of Tutankhamun's tomb in 1922 reinforced that there was a big, wide world out there ready to be explored.

This was also the golden age of film, with Hollywood producing silent movies oozing with high fashion and glamour. This influenced our homes with mirrored surfaces, cocktail cabinets and glassware for the opulent parties that ensued.

Interior design became fashionable with the birth of modernism. In Paris in 1925 the *Exposition Internationale des Arts Décoratifs et Industriels Modernes* showcased a new minimal style exhibiting streamlined, geometric art and stylized furniture in new materials, which complemented a new, simple architecture. Le Corbusier's work received mixed reviews; his minimalist designs of tower blocks, roof-top terraces and walls of windows was seen as revolutionary, heralding him as a true pioneer of modern architecture. However, it took until the 1930s for it to become mainstream and the 1960s before the phrase 'art deco' was coined.

In Germany the Bauhaus school was developing its own style of modernism that would influence the rest of the world for decades to come. After Germany's defeat in World War I, freedom of expression was finally encouraged after years of censorship. The Bauhaus school brought together art, crafts and architecture, which focused on simplicity, functionality and the ability to be commercial yet still beautiful.

The role of women in society was evolving fast. The flapper girl burst onto the dance floor with her new androgynous style, short boxy dresses and even shorter hair. She danced the Charleston, smoked in public and did things her way. In the UK in 1928, women finally gained voting equality with men and were released from restrictive Edwardian propriety.

All of this was against a backdrop of high unemployment and strikes. The world was heading for bust and in 1929 the American stock market in Wall Street crashed. This was to be the start of the worst global recession of the 20th century. The depression of the 1930s had a devastating effect on America with 25 per cent unemployment – it took ten long years to recover.

In the UK interest rates were cut, signalling the push towards home ownership. The falling costs of building materials and cheap price of land meant that the construction industry boomed, especially in the south. Three million new homes were built and by 1938, 35 per cent of homes were privately owned. Marriage rates began to rise with a real desire for security, contrasting with previous generations. Prices dropped, credit became available and with 600,000 people attending the 1938 Ideal Home Exhibition the long-term future looked promising. However, the world was about to change. On September 1, 1939 Germany invaded Poland; Britain and France declared war and the next six years altered our homes, our relationships and our lives forever.

The Kitchen

The 1920s/30s kitchen was small and functional, positioned at the back of the house. It consisted of free-standing units made from natural pine, often painted white. These would have pull-out worktops coated in enamel for practicality. Sometimes they would have an in-built shopping list so the housewife or maid could write down what was needed for the day ahead. New homes were designed with simple, fitted cupboards in white.

As the majority of people couldn't afford a fridge, food was bought daily from the local grocer, baker and butcher. Many homes had a larder, usually a cold storage room behind the kitchen, whilst poorer families stored their milk in a hole in the ground covered with a patch of grass to keep it cool.

The colour schemes were white and black with either lemon yellow or mint green accents. This matched many of the pieces of kitchenware of the time, which would be displayed on a dresser in more affluent homes.

The sink was an enamel Belfast or butler sink, large enough for all the washing up. Plates were stored in racks attached to the wall. Floors would be covered in linoleum. During the Depression of the 1930s most households lost their hired help so the lady of the house had to cook for her family and guests. New

homes had a hatch between the kitchen and dining room so that she could be the perfect hostess as well as the cook.

Time-saving gadgets were invented, including the toaster in 1925 and the electric iron in 1926. These were chrome-plated and industrial compared to our modern versions. Even though many homes now had electricity, most chose gas ovens as the more affordable and practical solution.

This 1920s/30s look is very popular now with many retailers reproducing the enamelware and ceramics to go alongside modern, pale green-fronted cabinets and rectangle brick-effect tiles. A 1920s/30s look filled with original vintage pieces is totally achievable and can be styled alongside modern appliances. Choose silver gadgets, tiled flooring and a ceramic sink to complete the look.

Must-have Items

STORAGE

The blue and white stripes of T.G. Green's Cornishware not only are a must-have for any 1920s/30s modern vintage kitchen, but have come to represent true Britishness for any kitchen, new or old. The range was first designed in 1926 in Derbyshire, UK and was applauded for the way it was manufactured. When made, stripes of blue glaze are removed to reveal the white pottery beneath. This makes the shiny blue stripe simply pop off the jar as it is raised. The name allegedly derived from someone's vision of the blue Cornish sea with its white waves. It was so successful that it was produced until recently with only a slight design change in the 1960s. The storage jars are probably the most collected, but they also produced rolling pins, plates, bowls and jugs. A yellow version appeared later, aimed at the American market, who preferred the sunshine hue rather than the cold blue.

For a real Art Deco look choose the Streamline range by T.G. Green. Produced in the 1930s it also has raised bands of colour, but this time they are a fine line. The ceramic is a cream colour with a slightly rounded shape and the lines are the traditional deco kitchen shade of green, coordinating perfectly with other pieces from this era. It didn't prove as popular as the Cornishware and so production stopped early.

British pottery manufacturer, Sadler, produced a similar range – Kleen Ware with green stripes – popular into the 1940s/50s. The colour is reminiscent of the utility china that would be in everyone's home only ten years later.

T.G. Green Cornishware, c. 1930s

T.G. Green Cornishware, 1960s

T.G. Green Streamline, 1930s

STYLING TIP

Cornishware should be out on display, especially on a dresser in a traditional way. Mix up the coloured stripes from the other ranges or contrast it with pretty pastels of 1940s utility china. Remember to use them in your day-to-day life. For example, the jug looks wonderful filled with yellow spring daffodils on a white linen tablecloth.

ENAMEL

Enamel kitchenware has been around since the 1700s, but it wasn't until the 1930s that it actually became fashionable. The inter-war housewife loved it for its easy to clean, non-porous finish, as well as its chic new look. As it came in a variety of bright colours, such as terracotta, green, blue and white and always with an alternative coloured edging, she could really start to coordinate her kitchen for the first time. However, its popularity declined in the 1950s when the easier-to-clean melamine was introduced.

Bread bins in light green enamel with black handles and BREAD written across the front adorned every kitchen worktop. To coordinate with this, families had flour jars and smaller matching tea, coffee and sugar canisters. Cookware also matched, with casserole tins and baking trays in cream and green. Colanders, ladles, milk jugs, deep saucepots, measuring jugs, kettles, buckets... the list is endless. The white versions became the norm in the 1940s, but this period definitely favoured green.

These items can still be used in the way they were intended even though they now will all have enamel loss and slight rusting. Remember, they have survived a world war and have bags of character so they deserve to be proudly displayed on your worktop.

RESTORATION TIP

The odd bit of rust on your bread bin is okay, but you will want to remove rust from inside a vintage enamel kettle or coffee pot. First, rub as much off as you can with soapy water and a sponge. Rub in circles on the affected area only and use a toothbrush to get into any tricky corners. Rinse out and dry fully. Mix two tablespoons of white vinegar with two tablespoons of baking soda, spread this onto the rust and leave for three minutes. Use the cleaned toothbrush to rub the paste in a circular action. Rinse, wash and dry fully. Repeat if needed, leaving the mixture on for longer each time.

Enamel bread bin, c. 1930s

Enamel tins, 1930s–1940s

Enamel tin, American, 1930s

STYLING TIP

All enamel items can have alternative uses. Why not use a flour jar as a planter for herbs and put it on your windowsill? A pitcher makes a great vase for spring tulips. The small bowls look great with eggs in, sitting on the worktop. Store your cleaning liquids in the enamel bucket to take around the house when you're doing the housework.

Watch Out!

Leaving water in vintage enamel will cause further rust. Empty coffee pots and kettles and dry with a kitchen towel in between use.

TINS

Advertising tins were made as early as 1810 and with the consumer boom of the 1920s they became hugely popular and are still collectable. Families bought new, exciting food products that often came in a tin, which was reused or displayed in the kitchen. Oxo, Lyon's tea and McVitie's & Price's biscuits were just some of the brands enjoyed.

Biscuit tins were made with glamorous images on the lid of ladies wearing the new fashions of the time. Cigarette tins also had women on, highlighting the shift in perception that even ladies could have a good time.

It wasn't just tins that had great images on; soap also had packaging with fashionable subjects as well as comical cartoonlike images, such as the Lifebuoy boxes. Soap flakes, such as Chipso and Ipso, were produced in bright coloured boxes with written captions almost popping out from the design.

STYLING TIP
Display vintage washing powder boxes on a shelf near your washing machine or to brighten up a utility room.

Biscuit tins,
1920s–1930s

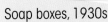

Soap boxes, 1930s

STYLING TIP
These small advertising tins look great made into a piece of art. Paint about six coats of magnetic paint on to a wooden board or a wall. Choose a perfect rectangle so it looks like a picture and perhaps frame it. The tins will stick to the paint and be on show in your 1920s/30s kitchen.

Oxo tin, c. 1930s

TEAPOTS

Stylish families drank tea from a silver tea service. Often made of silver plate, they were designed and manufactured in Sheffield, UK and had angular wooden or Bakelite handles reminiscent of ceramic teacup handles. Sitting on a silver tray with a matching milk jug and sugar bowl, the lady of the house would be proud for her maid to serve tea this way.

The rest of society was more likely to use a plain ceramic teapot with a chrome-plated 'cosy' covering the top. Designed to keep your pot hotter for longer, the milk jug and sugar bowl had matching cosies. Ellgreave Pottery, UK, led the way with their thermal-designed chrome cosy, which sat over a very plain, often pastel-coloured ceramic teapot. They branded it Heatmaster and developed the style, perfecting it in the 1950s. This later model is still very deco in style, but its atomic plastic ball feet are a real giveaway when dating it. They also designed an egg cup with a chrome-plated cosy top and inner insulation to keep your boiled egg warm.

RESTORATION TIP

Chrome plate can get scratched from use, but you can remove some of the lighter marks. Before you start, ensure the item is dry and at room temperature. Coat the scratched surface and a small piece of fine 0000 grade wire wool (steel wool) with chrome polish and gently rub in small circles to buff the scratches. Make sure no wire wool touches any non-scratched patches and that it is moist with chrome polish at all times. After a few minutes clean with a dry, soft micro-fibre cloth and check if you need to buff more. Gently repeat as necessary and then polish as usual.

Heatmaster teapot, 1950s

Heatmaster egg cups, 1950s

Silver-plated teapot, c. 1920s

STYLING TIP

Display vintage glass jelly moulds on your kitchen windowsill and plant herbs in each one to use while cooking. This will not only add colour but also, by using different shapes and sizes, will add character to your room.

BASKETS

Willow weaving was popular at this time as baskets were used on grocery shopping trips rather than paper bags. Willow has been cut and used for thousands of years and used all over the world to make shelters as well as the humble basket. A willow tree is cut back heavily to encourage shoots to grow, which are then cut and woven into different shapes. In the 1930s, 9,000 acres were grown on the Somerset Levels in the UK alone, but this has been in decline ever since with the introduction of the carrier bag and the shopping trolley. Pull-along trolleys were also loved for their convenience.

Shopping basket, c. 1930s

STYLING TIP

Store your linens and tea towels in baskets on the exposed shelves of free-standing units. Alternatively, store vegetables in baskets on your worktop.

T.G. Green Gripstand mixing bowl, 1930s

MIXING BOWLS

All cakes and bread would have been made in a ceramic mixing bowl by T.G. Green or Masons. They followed a classic style in a glossy oatmeal colour with a cream inner. The most practical was the Gripstand, which was a bowl with one straight side at the base rather than being circular. This enabled the cook in more affluent homes or the housewife to mix the ingredients thoroughly without risk of the bowl slipping. They came in various sizes and would be out on display for ease of access.

Watch Out!

Many of these bowl's inner bases have become porous over time and can easily chip. When buying ensure there are no chips inside the bowl as you don't want to lose some ceramic into your cake mixture!

TABLEWARE

Ceramics in the inter-war years took on a new, vibrant look, which echoed the overall mood. Brighter colours and surface patterns in geometric shapes represented the new freedom that was felt and pieces were shown off in glass-fronted cabinets and on dressers.

The most famous ceramic designer at this time was Clarice Cliff, whose work is respected and collected the world over. Born in 1899, she started work at the age of 13 and was given her own studio in 1927. This meant that she could decorate pieces with her own freehand style. Her first designs were orange and green triangles with black outlines and were called 'Bizarre'. These designs was made until the late 1930s and was shown at exhibitions around the country by ladies called the 'Bizarre Girls'. Her ceramics were sold through high-end stores, such as Harrods, which, unusually, earned her fame in her own lifetime.

The Shelley factory were also producing ceramics at this time, but were perceived as more elegant than Cliff. This was due to the quality of the porcelain and the less crude hand-painted designs. They featured the classic squarer shaped plate and triangle handles on teacups that really represent the style of the time, and was much copied.

However, in most homes simple hand-painted china was used to drink tea from. Many mainstream potteries, such as Phoenix, Old Royal, Cartwright and Edwards, produced tea sets and dinner services in similar shapes to the Shelley designs. Using the same colour palette of orange and yellow with black outlines meant that all homes could enjoy this new look.

Biscuit barrels were also designed with similar Art Deco designs. Clarice Cliff designed the stylized Crocus design on smaller versions that were used as mustard pots. They all had a metal lid made from a silver alternative called electroplated nickel silver (EPNS). Developed in the 1840s a thin layer of silver was bound to metal to create a silver look at a much lower price. Stamped EPNS, it is easily recognisable and was very popular in the 1920s.

Shelley Vogue shape cup and saucer, designed by Eric Slater, 1930

RESTORATION TIP

A crack left in ceramics will become worse over time so it's best to address this straight away. Place the item inside an oven on a very low heat to gently open up the crack. Mix up some epoxy-resin glue, which is made up of a resin and a hardener. Epoxy-resin dries yellow so you may wish to add some coloured paint powder to the mix. Mix equal measures together using a matchstick. Alternatively, use PVA glue. When the crack has opened, gently apply the glue over it. Don't apply too much: if necessary remove any excess using a cotton bud dipped in nail varnish remover. Apply masking tape over the crack and leave to dry. When cold, remove the tape. Any dried glue that has leaked can be carefully removed with a razor blade.

Old Royal trio, 1920s

Biscuit barrel with EPNS lid, 1930s

CLEANING TIP

Be careful when cleaning EPNS as it's easily scratched due to the thinness of the silver plate. Wash in mild soapy water and rinse. Place a sheet of aluminium foil in an empty sink. Half fill with hot water and mix in half a cup of baking soda. Place the item on the foil and leave for 15 minutes. The tarnish will break down and disappear. Rinse again and dry.

GLASSWARE

Coloured glass tableware was popular during this era, often in pretty colours, especially green. Sundae dishes, salad dishes with draining holes and cake stands all graced kitchen cupboards and were used for dinner parties.

They were made from pressed glass, a technique developed as early as the 19th century, where molten glass is pressed into patterned moulds to set. This method of production was quick and cheap, therefore perfect for commercial use, and was bought in its thousands. Queen Mary was a fan who bought for her personal collection at this time. Jobling Glass was a firm favourite with their opalescent glass, which was the same as that being manufactured in France at the time. They went on to manufacture Pyrex in the 1950s.

Cake stands were made from an opaque-coloured glass with a swirled edging and a silver-tone metal stand. They often had stars imprinted in the glass to give the cake stand a designed top. Some were also made in clear glass, with smaller versions for sweets.

Glass bonbon dish, 1930s

Glass cake stand, 1930s

Glass fruit bowl, 1930s

The Finishing Touches:

1. *Pie crust funnel* ☐
2. *Glass jelly moulds* ☐
3. *Ceramic blancmange mould* ☐
4. *Nut brown wooden rolling pin* ☐
5. *Enamel handheld candle holder* ☐

GET THE LOOK:
Annie and Trevor's kitchen, Northamptonshire

This kitchen is a joy, crammed full of vintage kitchenalia alongside modern appliances and pretty tins. The large kitchen table is clearly the hub of the home and is used for baking as well as eating. There are items from many eras here, from the 1920s through to the 1950s with one thing in common – pretty colours.

ANNIE SAYS:

My love of vintage stems from a life-long fascination with history, particularly social history and things that were used by everyday people. I have happy memories of spending time in my grandparent's home surrounded by pretty china, embroidered linens and 1930s prints. I love the idea of re-using, repairing and up-cycling pre-used items and find that vintage items are usually better made and better designed than their modern equivalents. Your home reflects your personality and I know I could never live in a home with no sense of history and be surrounded by things with no story to tell.

Colours are grouped together to ensure that items from different eras don't clash. Red enamel, china and tin sit within the free-standing cabinet, whereas the more pastel colours are on the dresser.

❚❚ ANNIE SAYS:

I have been influenced by the 1920s and 30s as this is the period of my house and I love furnishing my home with items from the period. I particularly love this era and the colour palette that was used. The traditional Deco green features heavily in my home but I also love splashes of red and yellow. Kitchenalia is something I love collecting, anything from the 30s to 50s, and I love the reds, blues and yellows that feature so strongly. ❚❚

The Living Room

The 1920s/30s living room came in a variety of styles. The affluent and design-conscious embraced the new Art Deco style with streamlined furniture in walnut with a gloss finish, which always matched. Shapes replicated the New York skyline or had geometric grooves within the wood. New materials were chosen, such as chrome and steel on chairs and table legs. Mirrored finishes were popular, appearing on tiles, table tops and cocktail units, as well as a large mirror above the fireplace. Even the walls were shiny, with sheen in the paint and on the wallpaper.

Most people, however, only dabbled with this highly polished look. In their newly built semi-detached houses with bay-fronted windows and stained glass along the top panels, their living rooms were a little more sedate. Walls were painted a pale matt colour or wallpaper was chosen in leafy patterns from the selection provided by the property developer.

Floors were either dark-stained floorboards or parquet, which would then be covered with rugs. A large circular rug, often with a swirled pattern, would be a feature under the low coffee table.

Homes were heated by electric fires with shiny steel surrounds. The living room had a coal fire with a tiled surround. This would be in neutral tones with a stepped, geometric shape that came in pieces rather than separate tiles.

The three-piece suite was introduced in the 1930s – boxy, simple and covered in leather or plain fabrics. Modernism defined simplicity with elegant yet functional principles and the living room furniture followed suit. Coffee tables had shelves underneath for your books and all units had doors so everything could be hidden for a minimalist look.

All homes proudly displayed their ornaments and glamorous ladies graced many a mantelpiece, either in bronze or porcelain. Lights were developing at speed as the electricity supply improved, with glass ceiling shades, tasselled shades on standard lamps, flush wall lights, up-lighters and down-lighters – the choice was endless.

This style influenced the 1960s look, which in turn has influenced what is in our homes today. Choose a chrome-legged table with a glass top, cabinet or sideboard with your things stored away out of view, a wood glass cabinet for your martini glasses and a simple feature fireplace. Team this up with a large mirror, eye-catching ornaments displayed minimally and contrasting geometric-patterned rugs.

Must-have Items

MIRRORS

Large Art Deco mirrors were a must-have focal point on the wall, with one in the living room, dining room, bedroom and even the bathroom. They were made from vertical strips of mirror fanning out to the sides, quite plain yet elegant. Often some of the strips were a coloured glass in black or green.

Most households, however, hung a smaller, more humble mirror over their fireplace. The choice for the masses was bevel-edged glass backed onto thin wood and hung from a chunky silver-tone metal chain. Some came with rose-coloured glass around the edges or with ridged, geometric-patterned metal adorning the top, however, a plainer version was more common.

Mirrored tiles were also popular, sometimes inset into fireplaces in clear as well as black and dark green. Pilkington Glass, UK, was the market leader with their revolutionary production methods for plate glass. In the early 1920s they worked with the Ford Motor Company, USA, to develop a process to produce sheets of glass that were ground and polished, making fantastic mirrors as well as glass for cars. Nightclubs and cocktail bars embraced this look with whole mirrored walls, which not only made small rooms seem larger, but also celebrated the reflection of a mass of a dancing young crowd. Furniture, such as side tables, was also covered in mirrored tops, often with twisted, bevelled edges.

Watch Out!
Check vintage mirrors for dark spots behind the glass. This is caused by moisture on the backing and can get worse, especially if hung in a bathroom. This can only be repaired by replacing the backing, however in many cases the stain will be on the glass too, which cannot be corrected.

Silver-plate mirror, 1930s

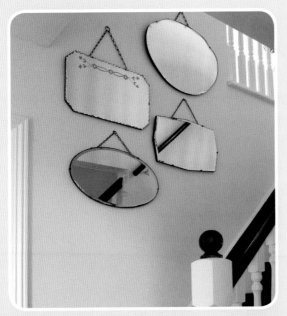

STYLING TIP
Hang a cluster of chain-hung mirrors in your hallway, running up the stair wall. This is not only eye-catching, but will also make a small space appear larger.

BARWARE

Prohibition in America from 1920–1933 dictated a ban on the commercial sale of alcohol. This drove bars and clubs underground with all-night dancing and of course drinking. In an age of decadence and celebration, the Art Deco design influenced barware with its geometric lines, mirrored accents and love of glamour.

Cocktails were the drink of choice, with European recipes enjoyed by American bright young things. Martini was a favourite, as illegal gin was readily available on the black market, and was served in a clear, angular glass. Champagne was also drunk, with complimentary bottles sent to tables along with coupe glasses. These open-bowled glasses oozed glamour, but the design caused the champagne to lose its bubbles more quickly and are not so popular nowadays. Babycham copied this style in the 1950s, wanting to replicate the opulent feel of this time. Decanters were used at home to store whisky and brandy. These too were angular in shape with matching smaller glasses edged with a gold rim.

All of this barware needed to be stored or hidden, so the cocktail cabinet was designed. Furniture makers in Britain led the way with designs in maple and walnut veneer with a glossy finish. Inside were glass shelves, mirrored backs, lighting and enough space for all your spirits.

RESTORATION TIP

Remove old liquid marks from decanters by pouring in warm water with two dissolved denture-cleaning tablets and leaving for half an hour. It is best to place a towel on the base of your sink to sit the decanter on, to avoid accidentally chipping the base. Rinse out fully then remove any stubborn marks by gently scrubbing with a baby bottle brush.

Uranium decanter and glasses, 1930s

STYLING TIP

Use a cocktail glass to serve food in at a stylish dinner party. A cold soup is a great starter to serve in the smaller styles. A delicious dessert in a coupe champagne glass is perfect instead of the usual sundae dish.

Cocktail glasses, 1920s

LIGHTING

By 1920, 35 per cent of homes in America had electricity; this rose to 65 per cent in 1930. In the UK, all homes built in the early 1930s had electricity as standard. With the introduction of the National Grid in 1933, whose aim was to improve the fragmented supply, families could finally enjoy fashionable deco lamps. It's worth remembering that many homes were still below the poverty line and would still have been using gas or oil lamps. Lightbulbs were now brighter, heralding a need for shades to diffuse the light back to the ceiling or down to the floor. Often these were glass – milky white to create a softer feel or enamelled in rich colours to match the interiors of the day. Standard lamps were popular with fabric-tasselled shades as well as desk lamps, such as the anglepoise.

Many homes had an alabaster pendant light – a glass bowl hanging on three metal chains from the ceiling. The alabaster mottled effect with splashes of colour within was practical and a cheaper alternative as the pendant light fitting could just hang inside.

The most iconic lamp from this era is a bronze or spelter lady holding a glass light. She usually sat on a marble base and originated from Europe. One of the most respected sculptors was Max Le Verrier who carved the Clarte in 1928 – a naked lady representing the goddess of light holding a globe. Interestingly, he used three live models to create what he felt was the ideal body shape – one woman for the head with a fashionable haircut, another for the feminine torso and an African-American dancer for the legs. This design has gone on to be reproduced time and again and can be easily found in modern lighting shops.

Watch Out!

Vintage lights up until the 1980s will probably not have modern wiring. Where possible you should buy a Portable Appliance Tested (PAT) light, but if you are in doubt get your retro lights checked by a qualified electrician.

Anglepoise desk lamp, later model, 1980s

Alabaster chain lamp, 1920s

RESTORATION TIP

The alabaster bowl lights are the easiest deco lights to collect as you will not need an electrician to install them. Many have lost their original fittings, but the hooks that go through the glass and the chain can easily be bought in a hardware store. The hooked plate that attaches the chain to the ceiling can be bought from a specialist independent lighting shop. However, if you cannot find one, an electrician should be able to attach it by screwing it directly to the ceiling using an S-shaped hook. Note: this must be done by a qualified electrician, as you could drill though hidden wires above the ceiling.

G·LASS

Glassware design came in many forms at this time with opalescent, depression, enamel, vaseline, pressed and cut glass being just some of the styles. The most recognisable of this time was opalescent glass, especially the works of René Lalique who exhibited in 1925 at the Paris *Exposition Internationale des Arts Décoratifs et Industriels Modernes*.

Lalique was a French glassmaker who until now was a renowned Art Nouveau jewellery designer. In the 1920s he developed his range of mass-produced glass made in metal moulds, however, his one-off pieces are the items that are highly collectable today. His designs resembled the opals that he used in his jewellery, a milky cream material with a sheen that can be softly coloured in pastels, such as pale green and blue. He designed vases, plates, figurines and even car mascots until his death in 1945.

Not everyone can afford a piece of Lalique, but he also designed perfume bottles including Nina Ricci's L'Air du Temps, which has two glass doves on the stopper. Small versions of these can be found today and will look great on your vintage dressing table.

In the UK, the Bagley Crystal Company was producing pretty pastel glass vases with an almost frosted finish. They were all pressed in moulds, but the handkerchief edging was done by hand. The popular pink colour was allegedly produced by adding arsenic to the mix, however, it was discovered that an innocent potato could make the same colour – no doubt a relief to the workers! In the 1930s they designed a glossy black glass range called Jettique, which was produced until the 1950s. All are affordable today and easily collected.

In America, depression glass made by machine and the almost glow-in-the-dark vaseline glass were popular. The latter was made by using uranium in the production; a mildly radioactive material that gave the glass its vibrant colour. However, during World War II America restricted the material to use in weapons only so the production stopped until 1958.

An alternative to glass are figurines made from metal or ceramic. Sculptures of naked nymph-like ladies with fashionable haircuts, racing cars or Egyptian cats all stood as individual pieces in the 1920s living room. The discovery of Tutankhamun's tomb in 1922 kick started our fascination with all things Egyptian as sphinxes and pyramids adorned everything. Germany was producing hand-painted porcelain figurines; a pretty dancing girl was the favourite with a coloured dress and slender frame.

Bagley frosted vase, 1930s

Uranium posy bowl, 1930s

Jettique Bagley glass, c. 1950s

German figurine, 1920s

STYLING TIP

Whichever ornaments you choose, give them the space they deserve on your shelf or cabinet. The 1930s way to display pieces was minimal so don't cluster different pieces together, but leave the figurine or vase to stand alone.

BAKELITE

The first plastic was developed in 1907 by the Belgian inventor, Leo Baekeland. Having moved to America in 1889 he worked on this invention believing that this new substance could change the face of design in our homes and cars. Made from phenol and formaldehyde, it was loved for its ability to be moulded into different shapes and in different colours. As a non-conductive material it also meant that it was the perfect housing for the newly designed radios and televisions.

In a dark brown or black colour, it resembled the glossy wood that was used at this time. However, because it was cheaper, an encased television cost a mere fraction of the price of one covered in wood. The wood needed to be made from several different pieces, cut to size and screwed together, whereas Bakelite was produced in one piece. This affordability made it the choice of the Depression era.

Bakelite was considered beautiful, plus the design could reflect the deco style with its curved edges and grooves following the same line. The US *Business Week* paper wrote in the mid-1930s, 'Modernist trends have greatly boosted the use of plastics in buildings, furniture and decoration, and contrariwise, plastics by their beauty have boosted modernism' (Penny Sparke, *The Plastic Age: From Modernity to Post-modernity*, London 1990, page 48). The patent ran out in 1927 resulting in other countries designing products from this wonder plastic. Philips in the Netherlands produced their own version called Philite to house their radio speakers.

Other products were designed, including clocks, kitchen utensils, plates and door knobs. There were smooth round ones, grooved raised ones and hexagonal ones made in black, cream, green and even red.

CLEANING TIP

Bakelite can become cloudy and scratched, especially on handles that are used regularly. Any item that is non-electrical can be cleaned using warm soapy water to remove any surface marks. Rinse and dry fully. Using a fine grit wet/dry sandpaper gently buff the scratched area. Apply a liquid metal polish in a circular motion using a dry cloth. Do this until all the marks have rubbed off and the item is a white colour. Take another cloth and rub the polish away.

HMV Bakelite radio, later model, 1950s

Bakelite clock, c. 1930s

Watch Out!

Identify genuine Bakelite by rubbing it with your hands to create some heat. If it's genuine it will release the odour of formaldehyde, which smells like carbolic acid.

TRUNKS

Foreign travel boomed in the 1920s, with the upper class holidaying on cruise liners, trains and even airships. In America it became easier for middle class couples to own their own cars; by 1921, over ten million people owned one, resulting in the need to invest money in the road infrastructure. A fascination grew for all things foreign and exotic, especially from Africa, with a growing trend for safaris. Ivory, ebony, tortoiseshell and mother-of-pearl all started to appear on handles for mirrors and cigarette boxes and on statues. Animal-skin rugs adorned the floor.

The one thing people always travelled with was a trunk or travelling chest. These were used for long-term travel as they held large amounts and were really sturdy. Large steamer trunks with leather detailing and smaller wooden-strapped versions were popular, with some even opening up to reveal drawers and a wardrobe section. Ladies travelled with vanity cases and hat boxes – a round leather box with a matching wrist strap.

RESTORATION TIP

To remove odours from the interior of a trunk, place a bowl of baking soda inside and leave for at least twelve hours. If the lining is badly damaged remove it completely and replace it with vintage wallpaper. To protect the outer canvas material for the future, paint it with a fine layer of clear polyurethane after you have fully cleaned it.

CLEANING TIP

The wooden exterior of a trunk is often dirty from years of storage, but can be washed using a mixture of warm water and a two capfuls of saddle soap. The leather details can also be washed in the same way. Be careful not to wet the paper lining inside the trunk, instead vacuuming this using a brush attachment.

Steamer trunk, c. 1940s

Hat box, c. 1930s

STYLING TIP

Not only do these trunks make great storage they also make perfect coffee tables. Place on a rug if you have wooden floors as the brass fittings may scratch. To protect the top consider getting some toughened glass with rounded corners cut to size – this can be done by a commercial glass cutter. Position four rubber blocks beneath each corner, with one centrally to ensure it doesn't wobble. However, if you want to use it for storage too then forget about the glass.

America really led the way with Art Deco furniture design even though they didn't exhibit at the 1925 *Exposition Internationale des Arts Décoratifs et Industriels Modernes*. A touring exhibition from the Paris show travelled around the States afterwards, which clearly influenced their future style.

The Austrian designer, Paul T. Frankl arrived in America in 1914 having studied architecture in Berlin. He lived and worked in New York and influenced by the city's skyline, he designed his furniture with this shape in mind. The Chrysler building was completed in 1930 and the Empire State Building in 1931. These giant skyscrapers influenced architecture as well as the city itself and Frankl's work took on these high and low shapes. His dressing tables had geometric sides representing buildings, with a large, rising sun-shaped mirror in the middle. His cabinets resembled a line of tall skyscrapers all at different heights.

In the UK, Lou and Harry Epstein designed custom-made pieces, which were not only popular from the 1930s to the 1950s, but also influenced mainstream design. They produced pieces in new materials, such as sycamore and walnut with a gloss finish. Their most famous design was the Cloud seat – a cream leather chair with a curved back and sides edged in wood. The idea was that you would feel like you were sitting in the clouds! They had a matching two-seater sofa as well as a dining suite in the same style. All the pieces were unfussy, curved with gentle detailing in beautiful wood. These of course were not cheap and ended up in more affluent homes. However, this styling filtered down to more mainstream versions made from light oak.

The three-piece suite was first designed in the 1930s, with families sitting on non-matching furniture before this point. They were quite low with very deep seats, rounded arms and covered in patterned material in greens and browns. Today, most have been re-upholstered in leather, which look great in modern homes and also fit in well with the 1960s look.

CLEANING TIP

Most of the furniture from this period was made from a veneer, which is a thin layer of quality wood attached to a thicker piece of cheaper wood. It therefore needs to be cleaned carefully. In a well-ventilated place, pour some lemon oil onto a cloth and apply to a small area in circular movements. When the area is covered in the oil, rub the cloth firmly in the same direction as the grain. Repeat this over the whole piece, a small area at a time, which should break down the dirt.

Walnut veneer cabinet, 1920s

The Finishing Touches:

1. Walnut mantle clock ☐
2. Geometric tiled fireplace ☐
3. Feature circular rug ☐
4. Bakelite telephone ☐
5. Bugatti car poster ☐

Leather sofa, 1930s

ANNA SAYS:

I love the style of 1920s and 1930s domestic interiors. I find the combination of modern styles in traditional materials, such as oak or walnut, very appealing. There is an elegance to this look that also fits very naturally into contemporary homes and how we live today. I live in a house built in 1926 and the original features still in the house are part of what has inspired me to style my house in this way.

GET THE LOOK: Anna and Steve's living room, South West London

A great way to add feminine touches to darker wood from the 1920s/30s is by adding tassels to keys. Here, Anna and Steve have chosen silk ones in the same eau de nil colour that is featured in the rest of the room. This echoes the tassels in the lampshades, and as many cabinets have locks, they are repeated around the room. Crochet tray covers add to this pretty feel as well as protecting the wood.

" ANNA SAYS:

I'm happy to have a big flat-screen TV in my living room, as I feel there is an authenticity about that in terms of how we live now. But I feel that works best if it is alongside a shelf of old books, or mounted in an old bookcase. "

The matching leather chairs with their curved styling and walnut edges are beautiful. Anna and Steve have re-covered them in a warm cream colour, which feels luxurious. Their modern television is out on show in the large bookcase, which is perfectly balanced without overpowering the elegance of the room.

The Bedroom

The 1920s bedroom was a feminine place with pretty, pastel-coloured accessories and soft furnishings against glossy wood furniture. The bed would have an eiderdown on top of bed sheets. The bedside table had a shelf for books as well as a lower cupboard. The focal point of the room was the dressing table or vanity unit with a large mirror and side drawers. Glass pots and perfume bottles would grace the top, alongside a jewellery box crammed full of costume jewellery. The woman of the house sat on a matching stool with leather covering. The whole effect was pretty and had a slight sheen to it, with a satin bed covering in the glossed finish often seen in wallpapers.

By the 1930s the bedroom would have looked more modern as Art Deco design became mainstream. The suite would now be made from a lighter wood with a darker coloured edging. New materials were introduced, such as chrome for the dressing table chair to complement large, silver metal-edged mirrors and bright lights. Many homes however, would not have had matching furniture with a glossy new sheen. Cast iron beds with simple quilts, sturdy wooden wardrobes and stripped floors would have been where most people slept.

This is a really easy look to achieve with any style of furniture, but works best with handmade wooden pieces or with modern mirrored ones. It's all about making the room pretty with an occasional chair in the corner, pastel-coloured bedding and of course a dressing table covered in sparkles. However, it's worth noting that this is definitely not a masculine look so you may need to reserve this for the spare room!

Must-have Items

FURNITURE

Lloyd Loom furniture is made from a special woven fabric that contains paper and steel. It is then applied inside a wooden frame to make curved chairs, tables and ottomans.

The American inventor, Marshall Lloyd discovered and patented this weave at the start of the century. Focused on designing prams (strollers) at first, he then tried his hand at furniture, feeling that this special material would be ideal. He joined forces with Frank Lusty from the UK in 1921 in order to introduce the range into Europe. They struggled at first as the British public couldn't understand that this was indoor furniture, seeing it as fit for the garden. However, when it successfully launched on ocean liners, London hotels and royal yachts, they were swayed. The company went from strength to strength until the factory burnt down during World War II.

Lloyd Loom designs make great bedroom furniture in a modern vintage home. Items such as dressing table chairs and laundry boxes, with their pretty colours, curved shapes and softer feel than the wooden alternative, are both affordable and easy to find.

RESTORATION TIP
To repaint your vintage Loom furniture gently rub down using fine-grade sandpaper in a ventilated area on a dust sheet. Vacuum it to remove any dust, then wash down fully and leave to dry. Spray on a coat of acrylic primer while wearing a protective mask. Stand about 30cm (12in) away from it and spray in even, sweeping movements. Leave this to dry fully and then spray a coat of your chosen acrylic paint in the same way. Leave to dry fully. Repeat as many times as needed. Seal the item by spraying with a sealant, again in the same way.

CLEANING TIP
The best way to clean stubborn stains from Loom furniture is with a toothbrush and mild soapy water. Rub the marks gently, trying not to get it too wet.

Lloyd Loom chair, later example, 1950s

Lloyd Loom side table, later example, 1950s

Watch Out!
If the Loom item is painted it is almost impossible to restore it back to its original glory. If you are buying one with bad flaky paint your only option is to sand it down and repaint it yourself.

DRESSING TABLE SETS

As in the kitchen and living room, pressed glass was also popular to accessorize the bedroom. Dressing table sets were made in moulds and mass-produced both in the UK and Eastern Europe. They consisted of a lipped glass tray with various lidded trinket pots and candle holders. Using uranium to create the strong green colour or in pastels, they oozed glamour at a time when women were expressing themselves with new bobbed haircuts and slinky fashion.

Handheld mirrors with matching brushes for hair and clothes sat alongside these dressing table sets. A new look was the guilloche backing – a swirled enamel effect that was replicated in plastic later. More affluent ladies used tortoiseshell sets, reminding her of foreign travels. A popular gift would be a powder compact, again with a guilloche-covered lid. Jewellery boxes made from the opal-looking mother-of-pearl would house her jewels.

Vanity set, 1930s

PERFUME BOTTLES

With the 1920s commercial boom, perfume sales rocketed. Ladies applied their perfume before a night of dancing, to feel alluring as well as individual in a time of new-found freedom. To reinforce branding, manufacturers designed elaborate and beautiful glass bottles filled with the scent. Naturally France led the way, with René Lalique designing opalescent styles for his own range as well as for cosmetic houses, such as Nina Ricci. Czechoslovakia also produced pastel- and amber-coloured bottles, with ornate stoppers that the lady would use to dab perfume behind her ears. The more premium styles were made from malachite.

The bottle design mirrored other Art Deco styling, with fanned strips of glass creating a geometric shape. An atomiser was attached to pump the mist across the neckline. Pressed glass bottles with matching powder pots were mass-produced for a more affordable version.

STYLING TIP

Store your vintage jewellery in cut glass pots and bowls on your dressing table top. Piles of clear rhinestones will add sparkle and give an air of opulence to your room.

Pressed glass set, Czech, 1920s

Glass perfume bottle set, 1930s

Glass perfume bottle, 1920s

CLEANING TIP

To clean perfume bottles and remove all the previous scent, empty all existing fragrance. Pour in equal amounts of white wine vinegar and water, replace the lid and shake. Leave this in for an hour and then remove. Half fill the bottle with warm water, some washing-up liquid and some uncooked rice. Shake and leave for an hour. Empty the bottle and rinse out. Leave to dry fully before pouring in perfume.

PICTURE FRAMES

Photography developed massively in the 1920s with the introduction of the first single-lens reflex (SLR) camera and 35mm film, both of which have influenced magazines and film ever since. At a time when living for the moment was paramount, taking a snapshot to remember what you did was very popular. Foreign travel, day trips to the beach, christenings and weddings were all recorded and then treasured.

Photo frames were therefore a must and would be displayed in the living room as well as the bedroom. Wooden frames designed in a fan shape to mirror the furniture were fashionable, with clear glass sections to slip your pictures into, as well as Bakelite versions.

STYLING TIP

For the wall why not frame 1930s fashion magazine covers to give your bedroom a touch of glamour? These can be bought from auction sites or from specialist retailers.

Wood photo frame, 1930s

STYLING TIP

Fast forward almost one hundred years and we now live in a digital world resulting in a decline in printed photos. Buck this trend and display your treasured images on your bedside table. You could gather old black and white photos of your family from this time too.

EIDERDOWNS

The bed would have had a silky quilt or comforter on top, above the sheets. They were gently padded with eiderdown and a quilted design was stitched into it to form shapes, such as flowers. Dusty pinks, burnt oranges and silvery blues were popular and added a real sense of luxury to bedtime as well as warmth instead of blankets. Patchwork quilts were also desired, especially those made by family members, lovingly passed from one generation to another.

Pink quilt, c. 1930s

CLEANING TIP

Vintage quilts can be carefully cleaned, but please don't put them in the washing machine! First, shake fully to remove any loose dust. Take the nozzle of the vacuum cleaner and cover it with a pair of nylon tights (pantyhose). Gently vacuum the quilt on the lowest setting. Fill a bath with lukewarm water and a mild washing powder with no chemicals in. Before submerging the quilt in the water, dab each colour with water to check that the dye doesn't run. If the test is okay then gently put the whole quilt into the water. Do not scrunch it up while washing or rinsing as this will disturb the feathers. Dry by pressing a dry towel against it. Gently lift it from the bath to avoid rips and dry it flat. If the dyes do run, you will need to wet a small cloth to wash and rinse each section individually. Dry in the same way as above.

The Finishing Touches:

1. Displays of ostrich feathers ☐
2. Floral-covered screen ☐
3. Round silk cushions ☐
4. Long-tasselled lampshade ☐
5. Leather suitcase full of love letters ☐

GET THE LOOK: Annie and Trevor's spare room, Northamptonshire

This bedroom takes me back to staying at my grandma's home; the cosy feel with pretty touches fills me with a real sense of nostalgia that makes me feel safe. This has been created by the layered quilts on the bed as well as great storage, such as leather suitcases and floral hat boxes on top of the wardrobe. I would love to stay in this room!

 ## ANNIE SAYS:

I love vintage textiles and have a large collection of eiderdowns as well as linens and fabrics. Eiderdowns are used on all my beds as they are wonderfully warm and lightweight; in the winter they are on sofas and armchairs as something to snuggle up to on a cold evening. I use vintage sheets and beautiful hand embroidered pillowcases, finding the quality far better than anything I could buy now. And I find them in charity shops for only a few pounds.

GET THE LOOK:
Anna and Steve's spare room, South West London

This bedroom, although filled with arts and crafts furniture from an earlier period, uses the green tones found in the original tiled fireplace within the accessories and bedspread. It is an elegant space with the crisp white linen and green pressed glass.

 ## ANNA SAYS:

For us, there are two key aspects to putting together a look from a specific era, as opposed to just a general 'vintage' look (although I find that charming too!). The first thing is to do research about how homes in that period looked – whether from watching films or reading books. Doing this means that anytime I come across something like a picture frame or a vase, I will know straightaway if it will work as part of the look I'm after.

ANNIE SAYS:

I have used the large wall space to display my collection of vintage 1930s classroom prints as well as Vernon Ward prints of Cornwall. I love the sea and have used this theme in the bathroom and in the vintage seaside prints and postcards on the landing.

GET THE LOOK: Annie and Trevor's hall, Northamptonshire

Instead of framing photographs to display on the top of furniture, Annie and Trevor have cleverly used vintage tins from this era. These are propped up so that the images are on show; glamorous ladies with authentic fashions and hairstyles from the 1920s become features rather than storage.

1940s—1950s

The world was at war until 1945 and times were incredibly tough. Rationing of food, loved ones away at war and fear of nightly bombings ironically brought a sense of community and a new type of freedom on both sides of the Atlantic. The Depression of the 1930s was over as women filled the jobs that the men had left behind. In factories and on farms, they were gaining a sense of independence never felt before, as well as learning new skills.

Government initiatives impacted on how people spent their spare time. The Make Do and Mend campaign showed us how to make shirts from old pillowcases, while Dig For Victory encouraged us to grow our own food in a time when produce was scarce. Factories gave up their materials and labour force to the war effort, so innovation and design stopped. European artists and architects fled to America, moving the creative hub to New York City. Hitler quashed all independent design in Germany so the key players in the Bauhaus school continued their work in America, returning home in the 1960s.

From 1946, construction gathered pace due to the need for new housing after the Blitz. Prefabricated homes were built at speed to create a new-look street. In America, suburban neighbourhoods were redesigned with front gardens and a white picket fence. The UK wanted to show the world that they could lead the way in manufacturing. The 'Britain Can Make It' exhibition organized by the Design Council in London set out to showcase this, with furniture designers such as Ercol showing their ability to design stylish furniture in new lighter wood, signalling a change in our homes.

While the 1940s were about austerity, the 1950s were about consumerism. Technology gathered pace with the introduction of the washing machine, the Polaroid camera and the computer. By 1959, 77 per cent of US households had a television. The Festival of Britain in 1951 exhibited radical new designs in fabric, furniture and homewares. Seen by a million people, the event helped to rejuvenate a broken London, with new tourist attractions built and souvenirs sold.

As interior design was growing, the role of women seemed to go backwards as women returned to the kitchen after the freedom enjoyed during the war. However, the kitchen was new, with bright, fun colours and a streamlined look.

The coronation in 1953 brought excitement to the UK nation as well as commemorative plates and tins. Whole streets crammed into one room to watch it on a small television set and street parties were organized, bringing at last a feeling of hope.

In 1957 the Soviet Union launched Sputnik 1, heralding the start of the space race that would influence interiors in the next decade. The Cold War was already underway, bringing an air of suspicion between the super powers.

By the end of the decade the teenager had officially arrived. The baby-boom generation born after the war were now ready to stand up and be counted like never before. Listening to records in their bedroom and jiving in their new flamboyant fashions, they signalled a real change in attitude just in time for the 1960s.

The Kitchen

The 1940s kitchen in most homes looked the same as those of the 1930s, with free-standing units, enamel storage, a large Belfast sink and a tiled floor. With rationing and women working outside the home, the kitchen was purely a functional room. Many had even given up their saucepans in the 1940s 'Saucepans for Spitfires' campaign and wouldn't own a new set until they got married at the end of the decade.

In the late 1940s fitted kitchens were installed in the new homes built after the war. These were basic compared to the 1950s version, although the heavy ceramic sink was replaced by a stainless steel one. Leading the way, American kitchens were designed with brightly coloured cabinets, such as red or yellow, often with glass knobs. This look would be embraced a decade later in the UK.

The 1950s kitchen moved from being a functional space to a social one, which the perfect housewife wanted to show off. Design was now about ergonomics with efficient layouts and labour-saving devices, as well as great colours. The units were always fitted with streamlined continuous worktops in Formica, a material that was celebrated for its easy to wipe surface and which could be produced in any colour.

White units were still available, but most households chose the coloured version, feeling that white was too clinical. The kitchen-diner was popular, with homes choosing to combine the old dining room with the kitchen to create a larger family area. Chrome-edged tables with matching chairs or wooden elm ones were popular and had one thing in common – a wipeable coloured top.

Gadgets were an essential item, with toasters, blenders and ovens all developed in shiny chrome. The most desired item was the washing machine. This saved housewives precious time, as previously they had to hand wash everything using a washboard and mangle. Adverts were launched that promised freedom to women with slogans such as, 'The neighbours are beginning to talk about me!' implying that the woman could now cavort around town due to the time saved by having a washing machine! However, in reality most women actually used a launderette until the late 1970s.

Patterned fabrics and wallpapers were fitted with images of fruit or Parisian scenes. A curtain would often hang in place of a cupboard door to hide anything that didn't need to be seen. Flooring would be patterned vinyl tiles, often with different flooring, such as parquet for the dining area.

Get this look by choosing modern cream kitchen units with a coloured worktop. Team this up with the same coloured wall tiles as the worktop to create a streamlined effect. Some modern cabinets have rounded edges that will add to the 1950s feel. A large American fridge, black and white vinyl flooring and chrome gadgets alongside vintage kitchenalia will finish the look.

Must-have Items

LINEN

Vintage linen had been made earlier than the 1940s of course, but this was the era for hand embroidering tablecloths, napkins and tray covers. Crisp cream linen was embroidered with pastel flowers and crinoline-skirted ladies to brighten up a plain cloth. Ornate patterns weren't produced at this time so making it yourself was the theme of the day. Alongside these, lacy doilies were made to use on the table, as tray cloths or even to hang on the back of your sofa. Add hand-painted china tea sets for the perfect vintage tea party accessory.

CLEANING TIP

Hand wash your vintage linen in warm water. To remove tea stains, treat the mark as soon as possible. Modern stain remover will work fine on vintage linen. Hang to dry then iron while still damp to remove creases, although a spray starch can also be used. It is best not to store linen folded as the creases can break down the fibres over time, so roll the cloths around acid-free tissue paper.

Hand embroidered
tablecloth, 1940s

APRONS

The 1940s housewife would have worn her apron or pinny for most of the day so it needed to be hard-wearing and practical. She wore a full length apron, handmade from off-cuts from other sewing projects. More of an overall, it would often be patchworked.

The 1950s housewife wanted a little more glamour in her new kitchen so wore a shorter half pinny, which made her feel less of a cleaner and still showed off her dress. These were cotton, often with a frilled edge and cute pocket.

Half apron, 1950s

STYLING TIP

These 1950s pinnies are too good to be stored away. Hang a few in a row from a set of hooks, coordinating with the colours of your kitchen. Alternate them with tea towels from the era.

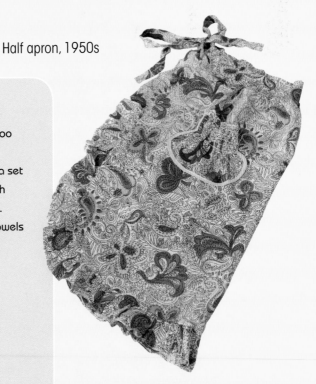

BAKEWARE

The 1950s love of baking was boosted by Tala kitchenware. They designed practical metal items, including icing cones, melon scoops, baking trays and the Cook's Measure. This was a dry measure made from enamelled metal in a cone shape. It was designed with various popular grocery items listed inside with a line that highlighted the weight of the item once the cone was filled. This made baking easier as flour could be weighed in seconds. Adverts appeared on the back of magazines such as *Ideal Home,* with the catchphrase, 'For Beauty and Efficiency', which were the two important features in kitchen design at this time. If you are baking using vintage cookbooks, then this cone is ideal as it measures in American cups, as well as ounces and pounds.

Tala bakeware, 1940s–1950s

COOKING UTENSILS

Skyline produced cooking utensils in the 1940s that had wooden handles. These were then painted in bright colours, such as blue and red with cream stripes. They originally came as a set with a metal row of hooks to attach to the wall. These were so successful that later versions were produced in the 1960s in orange, but by that time the handles were made from plastic.

Skyline utensils, 1950s

Watch Out!
The paint can chip off these utensils so try and buy ones that haven't already started to flake. Do not put them into a dishwasher as this will only encourage paint loss.

RECIPE BOOKS

The 1950s were the decade of brightly coloured cookery books. Aimed at the eager housewife, they ranged from recipes on baking to how to host the perfect dinner party. The early 1940s cookbooks often advised how to cook on a ration, but they did little to inspire dinner party menus until the arrival of Betty Crocker.

Betty Crocker was a cooking icon yet a fictional lady whose brand was first introduced in 1921. Throughout the 1940s the books became hugely popular, with Betty even being named America's second favourite lady in 1945, after the president's wife Eleanor Roosevelt.

In 1950 *Betty Crocker's Picture Cook Book* was released and became one of the most loved recipe books ever. For the first time the ideas were simple but also fun and the book was packed with advice on baking, such as a year's worth of cake ideas. It was full of glossy photographs, which was a new concept, and inspired all the cookery books that followed.

Recipe books were often distributed as promotional tools to encourage you to buy the ingredients featured. Stork produced small, simple books with whole menu ideas, McDougals wrote recipes using flour. Housewives would collect them then hand them down to their daughters.

STYLING TIP

Like all 1950s bakeware, these books deserve to be out on display. Their brightly coloured covers will add a sense of fun to your windowsill, but make sure the best cover is the one visible to everyone!

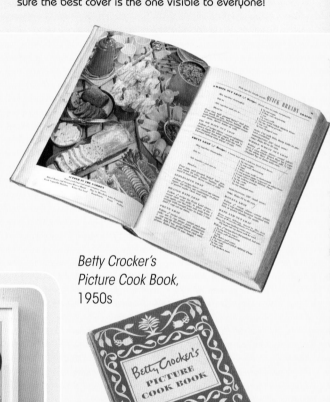

Betty Crocker's Picture Cook Book, 1950s

STYLING TIP

Frame vintage adverts to hang in your utility room. Often the back of popular magazines such as *Woman's Own* had coloured washing powder adverts with traditional images, such as Mother doing the washing and the children helping her. These will brighten up an often dull area of the home and bring a tongue-in-cheek smile to your face. They can easily be bought on auction websites.

1940S TABLEWARE

In the 1940s china production in the UK continued, but anything ornate was exported abroad. If anyone bought these styles they were usually factory seconds. Utility tableware was plain, nicely glazed, came in pretty pastel colours and was the choice of millions of Brits. Woods Ware made the classic pale green Beryl, which was the most popular – even used in schools and hospitals. They also made the lemon yellow Jasmine and pale blue Iris. Meakin made the pretty pink Glamour Rosa and Johnson Bros made the grey/blue Grey Dawn. They were practical, durable and can be easily found today.

Meanwhile in the USA, a similar style of tableware was being used. Anchor Hocking introduced their Fire King range in the early 1940s, which was also a pretty pastel green colour. The jade-coloured glass first became popular in the 1930s, but a decade later Anchor Hocking mass-produced it for cafes and restaurants who loved its durability and simple style. Often given away free as incentives to buy popular products such as oatmeal, the American housewife could collect the whole range while buying the family groceries. Building on this success they introduced kitchenware, such as mixing bowls.

Woods Ware Beryl and Jasmine teacups, 1940s

Johnson Bros Grey Dawn teapot, 1940s

Fire King Jadeite Alice teacup, 1940s

Watch Out!
While Jadeite is durable, it is not microwave proof!

STYLING TIP
These pastel shades look great out on display. Attach a plate rack to your kitchen wall and mix up the colours along the rack. Alternatively, if you have more space, display them on a dresser. Add the teapots, milk jugs and trios plus any other pretty vintage treasures you have. The blue striped Cornishware from T.G. Green looks fantastic with it. Remember to use them – they look even better with a slice of cake on a pretty, embroidered linen tablecloth!

1950S TABLEWARE

After almost a decade of plain-coloured china, people fell in love with modern patterned tableware that would become the norm in the 1960s. The most recognisable design was called Homemaker by Ridgeway, with its black and white hand-drawn images of fashionable furniture styles, aimed at young people setting up home for the first time. A Robin Day chair, a Gordon Russell sideboard and a boomerang table are sketchily drawn on the white ceramic. Designed in 1955, it became the first mass-produced tableware sold through Woolworths.

It wasn't just the patterns that contrasted with the previous utility and Art Deco styles. New shapes were organic and curved compared to the previous straight lines, with Midwinter leading the way. Having visited America in the early 1950s, they introduced their Stylecraft range in 1953. With bold transfer prints applied to the same styles, they created whole table sets that could be collected or given as wedding presents. In 1955 the Fashion shape was launched, ensuring that they became the leaders in ceramics well into the 1960s. Fashion designers even created ranges for them, with Sir Terence Conran's Nature Study epitomising this trend with its black and white colour and natural sketched images of insects and leaves. Other popular designs are Jessie Tait's zebra and polka dot patterns and Hugh Casson's Riviera scenes.

Fiesta Ware designed by Frederick Hurten Rhead was hugely popular in America in the 1950s. Launched in the 1930s, it came in a variety of bright, bold colours with a high glaze. The range saw resurgence in popularity after the 1940s with housewives collecting individual pieces in a mix and match fashion. An early catalogue describes the range as giving 'the hostess the opportunity to create her own table effects… Plates of one colour, Cream Soups of another, contrasting Cups and Saucers… it's FUN to set a table with Fiesta!'

Ridgeway Homemaker plate, 1950s

Midwinter Nature Study trio by Sir Terence Conran, 1954

Midwinter Cannes side plate by Hugh Casson, 1954

Midwinter Zambesi plate by Jessie Tait, 1954

RESTORATION TIP

To mend a broken handle on tableware you will need an epoxy-resin adhesive (resin and hardener). Mix equal parts together using a matchstick. This dries yellow so you could use PVA glue instead. Wash the cup and handle in warm soapy water and dry fully. Apply resin or glue to both ends of the handle and the round parts on the cup where the handle was attached. Any excess resin can be removed by using a cotton bud dipped in nail varnish remover. Use masking tape to hold it together while it dries.

Cover the cracks using the same method, smoothing over and leaving to dry.

Green Fiesta Ware pitcher, 1950s, with mini pitcher, 1980s

STYLING TIP

As these Midwinter designs are like works of art, hang them in a line on the wall. Alternatively, mix them within a wall of framed wall art for an eclectic look. You will need plate hangers to do this, which will need to be nailed to the wall.

PYREX

At the start of the 20th century the American company, Corning Incorporated, developed a new borosilicate glass that could withstand extreme temperatures. Originally designed to be used in railway lanterns, they soon discovered that this glass would make great bakeware when one of the executive's wives suggested it. It was branded Pyrex in 1915. A flan dish was launched and by selling licences to other countries to manufacture the material, this became one of the most successful kitchen brands in history.

In the UK, James A. Jobling from Wear Flint Glass bought the licence and redesigned the look of the pieces to fit in with current trends. One of the most successful periods for JAL Pyrex was the 1950s with their coloured bakeware. Casserole dishes were made in pastel colours with clear lids and white snowflakes and flowers adorning the sides. Replacing old metal trays, this new look made baking a pretty event, which fitted in perfectly with all of the modern kitchenware.

Watch Out!
Vintage Pyrex shouldn't be placed in the dishwasher as over time the heat and detergent will damage the painted surface.

Pink JAL Pyrex lidded dish, 1950s

Pyrex trio, 1950s

STYLING TIP
Pile up your coloured Pyrex on a dresser for everyone to admire. Colour coordinate the stacks and move from one colour to another to create a rainbow-like effect.

MELAMINE

Plastic became a kitchen staple in the 1950s due to improved methods of manufacturing. While Tupperware was changing the way we stored food, melamine crockery was fast overtaking bone china to become the tableware of choice; so much so, that families weren't just using them for their annual camping trips, but also for their monthly dinner parties. Traditional ceramic companies such as Midwinter even designed their own versions.

Melamine Formaldehyde was first designed before World War II in America and Germany. Respected for its durability, it could be moulded into any shape and made in bright colours. In the UK, Gaydon Melmex and Melaware designed their collections in the late 1950s and continued to be popular until the 1970s. At first they were quite expensive so were perceived as an aspirational, must-have item, but they were soon mass-produced thus returning to being merely a picnic range.

Melaware produced coloured sets in reds and greens with white inners. The shapes were free flowing with the handles organically growing from the cup. Gaydon was famous for its pastel shades, which coordinated with the pretty colours used in modern kitchens of this time.

In the US, companies were winning awards for their melamine or melmac as it's known there. Watertown's Lifetime range was introduced in 1946 and won such applause that it is still part of a collection at the Museum of Modern Art in New York. Like Gaydon's range, it was produced in pretty pastels. A firm favourite are the plates with kitsch flower designs that really sum up the spirit of the 1950s. Pink cups with white saucers covered in pink roses replicate the bone china versions without the risk of breaking.

Watch Out!

Melamine gets extremely hot in the microwave as it absorbs heat. It can be washed in a dishwasher, but the colour will fade over time, so it is not advised.

CLEANING TIP

To remove stubborn stains on melamine, make a paste using a quarter cup of baking soda and warm water. Gently scrub the stain using the paste on a wet cloth. Wash fully afterwards in warm soapy water.

Gaydon Melmex napkin rings, 1950s

Melaware Fiesta cups and saucers, 1950s

Watertown Lifetime rose plates, 1950s

STYLING TIP

These pretty cups and saucers should not be buried in your cupboards. Display them on open shelves, or better still in a 1950s free-standing unit. As these are perfect for children, storing them close at hand will look good and be practical as they can use them daily. Just like the utility china a decade earlier, mix and match the pastel shades, stacking them on the shelf.

FITTED KITCHEN

The must-have kitchen of the 1950s was an English Rose. Produced in Warwick, England by CSA Industries, it was hailed as an example of great industrial design. During the war the company stockpiled aluminium to produce spitfires, but afterwards found themselves with excess stock and a soon-to-be-unemployed workforce. To overcome this they designed a new modular kitchen with a metal frame that could be bolted together easily. Influenced by American designs, the end result was hailed as practical yet with a strong aesthetic. The curved front drawers enabled the 1950s housewife to have a deeper worktop without losing floor space. With integrated inverted handles, pull-out cocktail cabinets and a double stainless steel sink it paved the way for the modern fitted kitchen that we know today.

However, renovation isn't always easy. Sarah B. from North London had to pull her English Rose units apart completely. She describes how, 'Each cabinet was made up of about fifteen pieces, with the framework, plinth, metal inner and outer door panels, internal wood strengtheners, sound-deadening material, hinges, catches, stainless steel and plastic handles and so on. The fragile aluminium panels were badly dented so had to be straightened before being prepped for paint and re-sprayed pale yellow, rather than the original cream. Then everything had to be carefully screwed back together again before the kitchen was finally fitted.'

Restored 1950s English Rose cabinet

STYLING TIP

Re-cover your kitchen stools with new oilcloth in bright, candy colours. Alternatively, if you want a vintage covering, remove the vinyl top from an old ottoman, especially if it's ripped at the side. Not only will this recycle it, but will add a flowery pattern to a tired stool!

SARAH SAYS:

Restoring our all-metal 1950s English Rose kitchen was like working with a giant Meccano set, using the sort of techniques you'd renovate a classic car with. It looks great now, but people don't always understand the time and effort that went into getting it that way.'

RESTORATION TIP

Restoring English Rose kitchens can be done with dedication and vision. They need to be cleaned fully to remove all grease stains. They then need to be gently rubbed down ready for a re-spray. This can be done by spray painting or applying a powder coat. However, the best thing to do is take it to a car body sprayer. They will de-grease it properly and give it the excellent finish you want.

Most people had slightly cheaper alternatives in their kitchens as one English Rose kitchen cupboard cost more than the average weekly wage. They all had one thing in common though – fitted, streamlined cupboards and a Formica worktop. Many homes still used their free-standing kitchen units that had been in situ since the 1930s. These were bought as separates, often with pull-out worktops and sliding glass doors. Originally painted in pastel colours, families could embrace the new 1950s pretty or bright kitchen trend by repainting their old units. Often a matching drop-leaf table with a wipeable surface was chosen alongside elm stools with coloured vinyl seat pads.

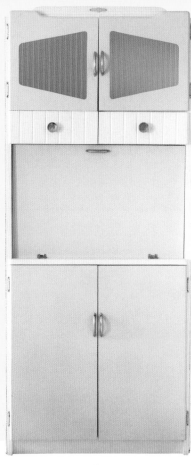

Restored 1950s free-standing unit

RESTORATION TIP

Often these units need to be repainted. The original paint must be stripped with sandpaper or with paint stripper. Fill any holes using wood filler. Finely paint it, gently building up thin layers using a combination of white or cream with a bright colour, such as red, or with pastels, such as pale blue. Line any stained drawers and shelves using vintage wallpaper in pretty florals to match the unit.

The Finishing Touches:

1. Chromed gadgets – blenders, toasters, kettles… ☐
2. Enamel scales ☐
3. Smith's kitchen timer ☐
4. Wire fruit bowl with plastic feet ☐
5. Flying ducks on one wall! ☐

STYLING TIP

Why not position a free-standing unit at the end of your kitchen and use it as a bake station? Store all your vintage mixing bowls, cake tins and flour jars here instead of in the usual kitchen cupboard. Make sure your prize pieces are out on display on the exposed shelves or behind the glass doors. Use the pull-out shelf to do your baking while dreaming of being a 1950s housewife.

Watch Out!

Many of these kitchen units have woodworm. Check all sides, base and back for small holes usually working their way up from the base. This can be treated, but if the wood is soft with a lot of holes it's not worth restoring. These units were often relegated to an outhouse in the 1970s so can be damp. Smell it before you buy it to make sure you really want to bake from this fixture!

CARLA SAYS:

We're inspired by mid-century atomic design and have incorporated different styles in our home, which reflect our interests and passions. We like clean lines, the use of bold colours and bright Formica patterns, the combination of brushed steel and quality woods. Our taste is very varied but the common link is the era in which our things were made.

GET THE LOOK: Carla and Martin's kitchen, Manchester

Carla and Martin have a rented modern kitchen but have added splashes of bright colours to brighten it up and give it their own personality. The 1950s red Melaware on the shelf alongside the silver Alessi juicer and the red atomic balls on the coat stand really pop out at you. The use of a free-standing unit acts as great storage, as well as tying in the vintage with the new.

GET THE LOOK:
Sarah B.'s Kitchen, North London

Sarah's English Rose kitchen is beautiful but was a labour of love. She has chosen two key colours in the kitchen, which are reflected through to the plates, appliances and kitchenalia. The pastel blue is perfect for the 1950s look as well as creating a bright, fun space. The low-level curtain hides the washing machine, which is a great trick if you want to hide some of today's white appliances.

" SARAH SAYS:

The vintage Prestcold fridge and New World gas stove came from house clearances. They are both British-built and work perfectly, although they are not very energy efficient. The pale yellow and blue fridge inspired the kitchen's overall colour scheme. I am currently restoring a huge 1950s O'Keefe and Merritt gas stove in powder blue that I imported from America, but the smaller New World has served me well for 15 years so far. **"**

SARAH SAYS:

I have collected the vintage kitchenalia such as canisters and crockery over many years. The cantilevered strip light is original 1950s, and the blue fibreglass lampshade over the table is a reproduction from America, as is the blue atomic wallpaper. The yellow metal lamps suspended over the stove are from Ikea

The table and chairs take us back to a 1950s diner. The chairs have been re-covered in atomic fabric that Sarah sourced from America, and then protected by a clear covering to make them practical as well as gorgeous.

The Living Room

The wartime living room in the UK was a dark, somewhat gloomy space due to the blacked-out windows. A government pamphlet described the dark curtains or blinds that should be hung, however, as money was scarce many painted their windows in black or dark blue paint. Low-wattage bulbs were used, and again to save money many hung cardboard boxes over the lights to dim them.

The dining table was often at the top of the Morrison air-raid shelter. This was a wooden framed box with metal mesh sides and a flat top, made to protect families during nightly bombing raids.

As paint and wallpaper were scarce, most homes had the same decor as in the 1930s. By the end of the war it was quite shabby and in need of a makeover. Some mixed white ceiling paint with dye to produce colours, but most went without.

The Utility Furniture Catalogue was produced for families that had lost their furniture during the Blitz or for couples setting up home for the first time. This described the oak wood furniture that could be made, which was very practical yet basic.

Post war, the living room changed radically. Many homes were built with a more open-plan feel, with the lounge combined with the dining room to create a social space. Furniture was designed in light wood on thin, splayed legs, which could be used in various rooms as room dividers and sideboards.

With the development of brightly coloured fabric with large repeat patterns, blacked-out rooms became a distant memory. Long abstract curtains without pelmets framed the large front windows, sofas were covered in smaller patterns, such as flecks and tweeds. Walls would simply be painted. Modern wallpapers with hand drawn-looking patterns grew in popularity throughout the decade, although many homes still chose florals and leaf patterns. Floors were wooden with a central rug or covered with a patterned short-pile carpet. Households fortunate enough to own a vacuum cleaner often took the brave option of a plain carpet.

Lighting was fashionable as almost all early 1950s homes had electricity. Glass shades were popular in tear-drop shapes with pull-down light fittings, as well as concertina-pleated paper shades in primary colours, desk spot lights and standard lamps with three separate shades. The television became part of the furniture, impacting the layout of the room as families now sat facing it rather than the fireplace. Fires were still coal, however, the fashion was for closed fires where the flames could still be seen. Many homes surrounded it with stone cladding and a shelf above for the mantle clock and ornaments.

This look is achievable with vintage or modern furniture, such as the reproduced G Plan range. Choose a light wood floor with large-patterned rugs, Venetian wood blinds instead of net and long atomic patterned curtains. Period features, such as picture rails and cornices, weren't fashionable in this era so this look works best in a more modern home either built at the time or more recently. Go bold with kitsch accessories – remember the 1950s is a fun look!

Must-have Items

BARWARE

In the 1950s, families loved spending a week at a holiday camp. Butlins was the favourite, with millions holidaying there every year. The bar was not only a place to relax and enjoy a tipple, but also somewhere that you could truly escape from British life. Often decorated as a tropical Hawaiian beach hut complete with hula girls and pineapple ice buckets, holiday makers chose to recreate this look on their return home.

Frosted, coloured glasses with gold rims in different shapes and sizes were bought to sit inside a cocktail cabinet. These had glass shelves with vinyl images and mirrors attached to the sliding glass doors. Families chose a free-standing bar with short, splayed legs. These often had compartments for cocktail sticks, holes for bottles and even inbuilt lemon squeezers for juices. On the top was a selection of accessories, such as a soda syphon and a fruit-shaped ice bucket, perhaps pineapples from Britvic, or apples and pears with glass inners and matching glasses.

Must-have items for the vintage bar are Babycham glasses. In 1953 there was a market gap for alcoholic drinks for young ladies. Men drank sherry, whisky and ale; women drank gin and crème de menthe. Babycham was perceived as fun, sparkly, aspirational; with the introduction of the deer brand image, young ladies found their tipple.

Metal pineapple ice bucket, 1950s

Atomic shot glass holder, 1950s

Babycham deer and glass, 1950s–1960s

STYLING TIP

If a complete bar isn't your thing, a vintage cocktail cabinet can have other uses. Display your vintage handbags in a glass-fronted one to keep them away from children's sticky fingers. Use a teak cocktail cabinet as a stylish bureau. The front-folding cupboard door is an ideal place for your laptop. Why not use a free-standing bar to hide your modern music: storing your record and MP3 players behind it not only keeps them out of view but your bar becomes a modern vintage DJ booth!

Watch Out!

Soda syphons need extra parts to work properly. A full syphon should come with a hose and extra sparklets to create the pressure to force out the drink. These can be bought separately, but ideally should be sold together; if not the extra cost should be factored into the price.

1940S FURNITURE

During the war timber was in short supply, but there was still a great need for new furniture to be made especially in cities recovering from the Blitz. To control manufacture, the government in 1943 outlined the exact specification for furniture made. In a time when bombed houses were being rebuilt and many newlyweds were setting up home, they formed a committee of influential designers to create the Utility Furniture Catalogue. This dictated the design, material and even which screws should be used on twenty standard items. The designs were simple and functional, alluding to furniture made during the Arts & Crafts movement. Cabinets sat on plinths rather than legs, handles were wooden as metal was scarce and most were made from strong oak or dark mahogany.

Even though the committee saw this as their big chance to influence the country with 'good design', most pieces were plain, looking to the past rather than the future. However, each piece was sturdy, substantial and of better quality than furniture produced a decade earlier. Such items have passed the test of time as they can still be found today.

Utility table and chairs, 1940s

Watch Out!
Look out for the CC41 stamp on utility furniture. This will be imprinted into the wood underneath and stands for Clothing Coupons 1941.

1950S FURNITURE

Enjoying a growing sense of optimism and freedom, we now demanded a new start in our homes. The utility wood was perceived as gloomy and the design drab. With aluminium, fabric and light wood becoming readily available again it seemed that a change was needed in furniture design.

In 1951 the Festival of Britain was a real turning point. Its aim was to create a feeling of recovery and inspire better design for the new towns being built. Eight million visitors came to see contemporary architecture, industrial and furniture design. Room sets were created, with modern furniture offset against the new fabrics and prints of the

RESTORATION TIP
If the table top picture has been damaged, the top can be gently lifted off to change the image. Carla and Martin from Manchester have revamped their table using glitter and heaps of patience.

Restored screw-on leg coffee table, 1950s

day. The wood had turned light overnight, with English elm and light oak being the favourites. Legs on all furniture were thin and splayed, making them seem to float off the floor. Chairs and tables were curved and traditional styles re-worked into the new look. Ercol was one of the key players with their simple yet elegant Windsor chairs, dining tables and sideboards. Ercol's elm is a great range to collect now as it sits perfectly in both a modern or classic setting. The iconic butterfly chair (1958), the nest of pebble tables (1956) and the day bed are items to look out for.

These new styles were labelled 'contemporary furniture' and for the first time since before the war the chair you sat on revealed your status. It was quite expensive so in reality only middle class families bought it, with the higher classes preferring Heals and Harrods. Large furniture retailers chose not to sell it as traditional styles were commercially more popular, so it was left to the independents.

The alternative was the original 'flat-packed' furniture, with kits available so you could build your own. These were primarily coffee table tops with shiny black screw-on legs and metal feet. A classic shape is the kidney side table with three tripod-angled legs. Often the tops were laminated in a marble or wood effect, but the more flamboyant chose picture scenes. Maps, flowers and even kitsch flamingo paper pictures were cut to fit under a thick, clear plastic covering. They were modern, light and fun to contrast with the heavy wood furniture that came the decade before. These black legs can be found on all types of furniture, from sewing boxes to room dividers and are a key look, with even modern furniture now beginning to allude to this feel.

RESTORATION TIP

To restore Ercol furniture you will need to strip it all back to the original wood. Do this in a ventilated area, wearing protective glasses and mask. You need to remove the top coat by hand with a cabinet scraper, then sand it fully with fine grit sandpaper. You should now have a clean wood that looks natural. Apply two coats of sealer, waiting for it to dry fully between coats. Spray with two layers of a satin pre-catalysed lacquer. Again, wait for it to dry fully between coats. Follow the same directions for darker-stained items, spending more time stripping it back. Alternatively, take it to a professional furniture restorer.

Ercol Quaker chair in English elm, later model, 1960s

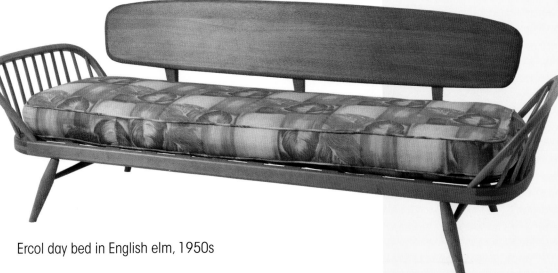

Ercol day bed in English elm, 1950s

TEXTILES

The 1950s saw an explosion of pattern after the more conservative prints of the 1940s. During the war there was a shortage of yarn and dye so there were strict rules on what could be produced. The number of colours used was restricted to four and the repeat pattern had to be small to reduce wastage during manufacturing.

After 1951, homes celebrated contrasting designs and colours on the curtains, carpets and walls in reds, yellows and blues. These textiles were seen as modern, with abstract shapes, strong repeat patterns and often almost blurry images, especially on florals. The patterns featured on new fabrics, such as spun rayon and barkcloth. Curtains were floor length and unfussy, sofa fabrics tended to be woven with a few coloured flecks and walls – if painted – were bright, picking out a hue from the curtains.

Leading textile designers, such as Lucienne Day and David Whitehead exhibited their work at the Festival of Britain. Day won awards for her designs, which primarily drew upon plant forms. Some say that she was the first person since William Morris to produce repeated intricate and popular patterns inspired by nature, however, she cleverly made them modern. In a time of re-growth her designs not only represented growth, but also took inspiration from abstract artists, such as Miró and Klee. Her textiles were affordable, allowing everyone to embrace this new look while having a piece of art in their living room.

STYLING TIP

Frame off-cuts of fabric to create great pieces of art. Sew the fabric to a linen backing so it hangs firmly in place. Attach double-sided tape to the linen not the fabric (so the vintage fabric isn't damaged) and attach to the inside of the frame.

Watch Out!

Vintage fabric can deteriorate due to how it has been stored. Check for odours, sun damage and thinner patches, which will tear easily. If buying online, ask the seller for details on the condition of the fabric.

STYLING TIP

Vintage fabric and wall coverings are hard to find, but many companies are re-releasing original designs, such as Sanderson's 1950s range. Hang vintage wallpaper on a feature wall and pick out a key colour from the design for the furniture. Vintage fabric can be bought in square metres – perfect for homemade cushions or stool covers. A good upholsterer or seamstress can help with this.

David Whitehead fabric, 1950s

KITSCH COLLECTABLES

With the increased affluence in the 1950s, families started to buy more frivolous items for their mantelpieces. Some were souvenirs from trips abroad, some were more sentimental and others just brought a smile to their faces.

The ceramic cat with its elongated neck was very popular. These were made in the UK, West Germany, Italy and the USA as ornaments, vases and even lamps. In the USA, Lane & Co produced the cat lamp, which sat on television sets around the country. The television was considered a piece of furniture rather than a gadget so placing your knick-knacks on it seemed perfectly normal.

The Italian Murano glass fish was another popular item. With coloured splashes and a marbled effect within its clear glass, it graced many a living room.

Chance Glass produced their first handkerchief-edged bowls in the UK in this decade, continuing late into the 1980s. Based on the early Italian Murano style, these contemporary versions captured the spirit of the 1950s with candy colours and kitsch patterns. They were also mass-produced with set patterns (gingham, polka dot, swirls, stripes and textures) available in a variety of colours.

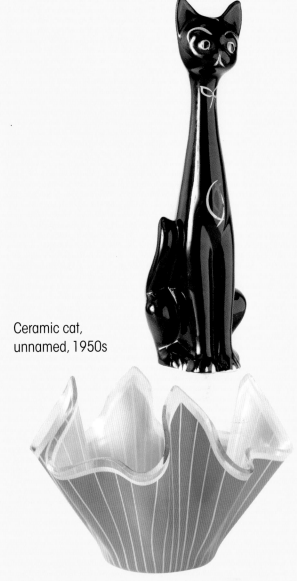

Ceramic cat, unnamed, 1950s

Chance handkerchief vase, 1950s

Murano glass fish, 1950s–1960s

TELEPHONES

The revolutionary design of the Ericofon or Cobra phone brightened up Swedish homes from the late 1940s and was introduced to the US market in 1956. The cobra, designed by Ericsson was the first marketed phone incorporating the handset and dial together (maybe a forerunner of the modern mobile phone) and came in 18 funky colours, but interestingly, never black. Its objective was to be lightweight, easy to use and to appeal to the commercial sector. The main customers in the early years were hospitals, who felt it was easy to use from your sick bed.

By contrast the UK continued with the serious black Bakelite phone well into the early 1960s. Designed in the 1930s, these heavy phones were the first to be accessible to all. By the 1950s they were produced in cream, red and green, but these were very rare.

Watch Out!

The Ericofon was mainly produced in the USA and Scandinavia. Make sure when buying that it has been converted to be able to work in a British system. This can usually be done by specialists, but you will need to factor this into the price.

Ericofon dial, 1950s

Ericofon, 1950s

Bakelite phone, 1940s

PLANT TABLES

Designed in Western Europe the tiered plant table sums up the quirky, ground-breaking design of the 1950s. Made from a dark wood with small circular-shaped tables covered in pretty coloured Formica tops they were designed to sit a separate plant pot on each surface.

STYLING TIP
Choose a 1950s plastic plant pot for each shelf. These look great in feature areas, such as in small alcoves or under a window on the landing. Give the space around them that they deserve for a real stand-out effect.

Wood plant table, 1950s

MOLECULAR SHAPES

The Festival of Britain in 1951 wasn't just about great design, it was also about science. Displays in the Dome of Discovery revealed for the first time molecular structures explaining our universe and this was seen by millions. The science behind what would be achieved in the next decade in turn inspired our interiors in this decade. The love of space and all things unknown was becoming a fascination and these atomic molecules were replicated as ball feet on many home accessories.

Starting off as painted wood balls, they were quickly replaced by primary-coloured plastic as people looked for more durable items. Magazine racks, coat stands, record racks, shot glass holders, planters and even waste-paper bins were all adorned with these ball feet.

Umbrella stand, 1950s

Coat hooks, 1950s

STYLING TIP

As these were designed with primary-coloured ball feet, they look great in children's rooms. Attach hooks on the wall to hang their gym bags from, store comics in magazine racks or use a planter as storage or as a waste paper bin.

The Finishing Touches:

1. Vernon Ward flamingo prints ☐
2. Three-glass shade light ☐
3. 1953 Coronation memorabilia ☐
4. Sofono heater ☐
5. Vinyl footstool on atomic legs ☐

GET THE LOOK: Carla and Martin's living room, Manchester

The West German plant stand has inspired the whole space; the red and yellow colours have been mirrored in the Sanderson fabric on the Ercol sofa and footstool. The atomic theme is continued on the ceramics, the splayed legs on the coffee table and an amazing American ice bucket.

" CARLA SAYS:

*Tiki and lowbrow have a major
influence in our lifestyle and on how
we decorate our home. We are both
design enthusiasts with a passion for
50s Americana, rock 'n' roll music and
Tiki culture. In a way it's, 'Mad Men goes
to Hawaii'.* "

GET THE LOOK: Sarah B.'s living room, North London

The living room is separated from the kitchen/diner by using a room divider. This means whether you are sitting on the sofa or cooking the dinner you can see the Homemaker ceramic tableware proudly out on display. These were popular in the 1950s and made up until the 1970s.

SARAH SAYS:

I found the room divider at an antique dealer in Antwerp, Belgium – apparently it's French. I rearranged it in two sections; as a one-piece unit it would have been too long for the lounge. Its glass-door cabinets are the perfect place to display my collection of 1950s Homemaker china.

SARAH SAYS:

My father made the TV table when he was a schoolboy in the 1950s, and the reproduction 'bullet' planters are from a company in Texas. The metal wall art is from Habitat: I'm always on the lookout for vintage-style items in modern home stores that will work nicely in my home – Heals and Ikea are also favourites. I found the various lamps and many of the decorative pieces at vintage dealers in California, Nevada and Arizona during various 'vintage buying' road trips, as well as on eBay, although I've had some of the pieces since I first started collecting 1950s stuff as a kid.

The colours here are pastel pink and blue – from the cushions to the lighting, everything matches beautifully. The pink colour is then echoed in the glass bricks which are used as a feature window as well as framing the entrance to the rest of the house.

The Bedroom

Like the kitchen and living room, the 1940s bedroom looked the same as in the 1930s. Dark to medium wood bedroom furniture, cast-iron beds, satin feel eiderdowns, patterned curtains and pastel-coloured walls were the key features. Windows may have been blacked out with dark curtains or blinds, so overall the look was quite sombre. Some homes would have bought utility furniture in oak with simple styling.

In the late 1940s and throughout the 1950s the bedroom changed dramatically for the first time ever. It became lighter, with suites matching the style of the rest of the home – pale wood with splayed legs. Curtains would be patterned, featuring large repeats, and walls were painted one colour or were covered in wallpaper with a smaller pattern on. However, the colours were prettier than in the living room and kitchen, with pastel pinks and baby blues being the favourites.

With the arrival of 'the teenager' the bedroom was used as a place to spend time with friends rather than just to sleep in. Therefore it was filled with accessories that they would want to show off, such as record players, phones and posters of pop stars.

Newly married couples setting up home spent time and money on creating a romantic space. They chose candlewick bedspreads, which seemed cosier than the satin that came before, as well as matching cushions and light shades. Even dressing tables had pleated, draped curtains underneath to hide toiletries, adding to the soft, feminine style.

Either look is achievable in a modern bedroom space. Hang reproduction or vintage wallpaper on a feature wall – behind the bed works best. A matching suite, pastel soft furnishings and an ottoman with a floral lid will add a feminine style. For a more masculine look choose early G Plan furniture with black screw-on legs and a bolder colour, such as turquoise or purple.

Must-have Items

RECORD PLAYERS

In the late 1950s the portable record player, with its hinged lid and carry handle, changed teenagers' lives forever. Sitting in their bedrooms with all their friends, dancing to rock 'n' roll and comparing vinyl, gave them a sense of belonging and increased popularity due to the size or content of their record collection. Singles were loaded in stacks to ensure continued play, with the Dansette record player being the most popular. Before this all music was listened to on the family's gramophone downstairs. Produced from 1951 until the late 1960s, Dansettes sold over a million units across the UK and they forged the way for other portable record players.

RESTORATION TIP
Dansettes and other similar portable record players can be reconditioned for the modern world, with the ability to play MP3 players. This can be done by specialists (see the Directory at the back of the book).

Dansette Popular, 1960s

STYLING TIP
Adding a set of black atomic splayed legs to the base of a portable record player turns the unit into a piece of furniture, to take pride of place in a corner of the room. Some already came with legs, but many have been lost over the years. You can buy legs and back plates as separates or remove them from an old, worn 1950s table.

THE DRESSING TABLE

A dressing table or a vanity table was an essential piece of furniture in the 1950s bedroom. A lady would take the time to sit at the mirror to apply her make-up, style her hair and select her jewellery. Her appearance was important in a time when pleasing your husband was paramount.

The dressing table would usually be a plain piece of furniture compared to the fun living room style, reminiscent of a desk with a mirror attached. On it she would have her perfume bottles and a handheld mirror set, which often had petit point stitched flowers behind glass and looked very feminine. Alternatively, pink plastic sets with kitsch patterns were chosen especially for younger girls. Jewellery was stored in a jewellery box with a musical spinning ballerina inside. Often given as gifts to young girls, they were kept for years standing in pride of place, adding a real touch of femininity to an often minimalist room.

STYLING TIP

These vintage dressing tables make great desks when the mirrors are removed. As the trend of working from home increases, choose one to create your modern vintage study. You can then hang the mirror in your bedroom or hallway!

Vogue vanity set, 1950s

STYLING TIP

Why not use a 1950s sewing box to store all your vintage costume jewellery? Choose the classic wooden cantilever style with pull-out drawers, or go for a Scandinavian style with a pull-back shutter-style lid. Each style has small compartments for all your little treasures and looks great sitting in a corner.

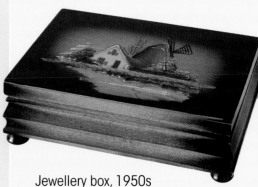

Jewellery box, 1950s

GROOMING GADGETS

New technology wasn't just for the kitchen in the 1950s. The bedroom also enjoyed a new level of technology, especially with hairdryers. Handheld hairdryers were first produced in the 1920s, but they were heavy and noisy as the motor was similar to the one in a vacuum cleaner. By the 1950s, companies had re-worked this early design to create a lighter, quieter, more efficient version. Pifco, established in 1900 in Manchester, UK, led the way with their handheld Princess model. Designed in 1958 it came in a variety of pretty colours, such as pastel pink and baby blue.

Pifco made a variety of grooming gadgets that came in fantastic packaging. The electric trouser presser, the heat massager and electric shaver all revolutionised our beauty routines at a time when looking good was a priority.

STYLING TIP

The packaging alone makes great props to sit on a shelf in your bedroom or bathroom. Don't worry if the boxes are a little worn as it all adds to the vintage charm. If displaying in a bathroom, be careful of excessive steam as this will make the cardboard damp. Mix with old bottles of perfume for that glamorous boudoir feel.

Watch Out!

These products all have old plugs so shouldn't be used without consulting an electrician first.

Pifco trouser presser, 1950s

Morphy Richards hairdryer, 1950s

The Finishing Touches:

1. Curved teak mirror ☐
2. Chenille bedspread ☐
3. Vintage wallpaper on a feature wall ☐
4. Folding alarm clock ☐
5. Dressing table stool ☐

GET THE LOOK: Justin and Adelle's bedroom, Todmorden

Forget wall art when you have a great vintage handbag collection! These structured bags work brilliantly hanging above the bed and add a real splash of colour, contrasting with the wood in this room.

❚❚ JUSTIN SAYS:

Adelle has a vintage handbag addiction! Favourite ones are hung on the bedroom wall – their various shapes, colours and materials make a great display and they're always at hand when putting together an outfit! ❚❚

GET THE LOOK: Sarah B.'s bedroom, North London

The light wood furniture is made by Haywood-Wakefield and is from the 1949–1951 Kohinoor range. These American pieces are really collectable and Sarah is lucky to have them. She sourced them in California and then had them shipped to the UK.

SARAH SAYS:

I chose a slightly kitschy 1950s oriental theme for the bedroom decor, with vintage wall plaques, lamps and statuettes in keeping with the styling. The colour scheme is lilac, turquoise and pistachio green, with reproduction abstract leaves wallpaper and atomic fabrics.

1960s–1970s

The 1960s were a time of great optimism. Children born after the war were now teenagers and were ready to shake off the old-fashioned ways of their parents. Everything around them was changing: Martin Luther King was showing the world that a person's civil rights were paramount, women were uniting to demand equality and Elvis was continuing to rock the jailhouse down.

Teenagers were discovering new fashions, music and hope. By the end of the decade they were moving out, going to college and buying into a new, young design for their shared homes. Their parents were enjoying not having to worry about rationing and were working out how to spend their credit. They invested in new kitchens and matching teak furniture, hosted cocktail parties for their neighbours and travelled on package holidays. They could begin to afford new gadgets and were enjoying keeping up with the Jones's.

The Space Race was in full force and influencing interior design at great speed. Furniture, lighting and even ceramics were becoming cosmic shaped. People were questioning religion and experimenting with new Eastern faiths, just at the time that The Beatles travelled to India and hippies to Woodstock. This impacted our home style as we moved towards a brighter, more psychedelic vibe. Orange was the colour of choice. The Bauhaus movement – quashed by Hitler – was reinvigorated in West Germany and organic sculptural ceramics and furniture design was once again celebrated.

The shape of our homes was changing too. Skyscrapers and tower blocks were erected, influenced by Le Corbusier back in the 1920s. Homes in the UK were being built at great speed with many families finally purchasing their own. The long and low ranch house was the popular choice in the US.

The 1970s, however, was a decade of opposites. The mid-1970s were a tough time economically and Britain found itself in deep recession with high inflation and unemployment rates. The coal industries were striking, driving up the price of electricity to an all-time high. At one point commercial businesses were only allowed to trade for three days a week and even television closed down at 10.30pm. This was mirrored in the US with rocketing oil prices. The slogan of the time was 'Don't be Fuelish', with its universal call to save energy. Because of this, our investment in home interiors was not a priority.

In tough times we always seem to look to the past for inspiration. Now we looked back to the Arts & Crafts movement of the late 1800s, with the fabrics of William Morris and the prints of Toulouse Lautrec becoming popular in their autumnal muted tones. The colour choice reflected the mood of the times – we had moved from zingy orange to dark brown.

The baby-boom generation had now set up home and were having families. Their home style had grown up too as they had new dinner services and matching tea sets. Received as wedding presents, they were perfect for the new trend of staying at home and hosting dinner parties.

Amid these tough times the world was still discovering new gadgets and time-saving devices. Computers, videos, microwave ovens and of course the Teasmade were all life-changing purchases in this decade. It almost feels that in between the demonstrations and dinner parties we were getting ready for the explosion of colour that was the 1980s.

The Kitchen

The fitted kitchen was designed in the late 1940s, but it took until the 1960s for it to become mainstream. The fashion was now wood, with cabinets covered in a thin wood veneer in medium to dark shades. The alternative was to paint the wood yourself, with pale blue being a popular choice. The emphasis was still on efficiency, with streamlined worktops and all appliances being nearby. Handles were inverted plastic circles, which were then replaced by strips of silver aluminium at the top of doors in the 1970s. Breakfast bars and islands were built with vinyl-covered bar stools underneath, making the space more sociable than ever. Whole walls were tiled, often with different patterns. A favourite was wipeable, tiled-effect wallpaper, which could easily be changed to update your room.

Some families embraced the Victorian look, popular at the end of the 1960s, with copper accessories, such as kettles on top of the units and copper pans hanging on the walls.

By the end of the decade most kitchens were white with zingy-coloured accessories in yellow and orange. Pull-down lights, wallpaper, clocks and utensils all coordinated, although by the 1970s the colour palette changed to more muted tones of brown and beige.

Floors were covered in vinyl tiles, which replicated ceramic ones, complete with mock grout. Venetian blinds hung from the windows. Inside the cupboards were great storage ideas, such as pull-out baskets – still commonly seen today.

The most life-changing invention of the 1970s was the freezer. Before now all frozen food was kept in the small compartment at the top of the fridge, but with the new under-counter or chest freezer, the family could have pre-prepared food every night. This really revolutionised the housewife's life as now she didn't have to buy food daily, giving her time to work outside the home.

This look is easy to achieve now as wooden units are sold everywhere. Why not choose a brightly-coloured kitchen door, such as orange, to really get the style and then team with retro accessories? Alternatively, choose cream gloss doors and edge them in a dark wood panel end. Hang a pull-down glass light fitting above your breakfast bar, which can be used only when you're sitting there. Accessories should be out on display: ceramic tea and coffee canisters positioned in a row near your kettle and cooking utensils hanging on the wall.

Must-have Items

TABLEWARE

After the curved shapes of the 1950s, ceramics in the 1960s took on another new shape. Midwinter, who designed the Fashion shape a decade earlier, now produced sleeker, straighter-lined coffee pots called the Fine shape. With geometric patterns, such as the Focus range or the abstract lines of the Sienna range, this was a more serious look suited to the style-conscious baby-boomers.

J&G Meakin's ceramics became an iconic look for this decade with its even taller and sleeker coffee pot. It stood proud on the table with its extra-long, elegant spout and high top lid. Taking influence from Portmeirion's range with a similar shape, this range became a must-have set. Whether covered in sensible circles or funky flowers there would be a style for every home.

By the 1970s, tableware matched the mood of the nation. In brown tones, Hornsea produced tea sets and tableware with textured flowers on. The ridged circles are reminiscent of the Fiesta range of the early 1950s without the pretty colours. They also produced mugs, heralding the move away from teacups and saucers.

Ironically, amongst all of these new modern shapes, the most successful ceramic of the 1960s was the traditional Old Country Roses. Produced by Royal Albert in 1962, this 22 carat gold-edged, pink rose bone china has become the bestselling range of all time. Based on a 1921 design, they went on to sell over 100 million pieces worldwide. Still highly collected today, it was mass-produced for anyone desiring a sense of nostalgia in a decade of mass change.

Midwinter Sienna jug and tureen by Jessie Tait, 1962

J&G Meakin Sunflower coffee pot and coffee cans, 1960s

RESTORATION TIP

To mend a chip in ceramic you will need epoxy putty, which comes in two parts – resin and hardener. Mix equal parts together using a matchstick. As this dries yellow you will need to mix in some powdered paint in the same colour as the plate. Wash the item in warm, soapy water and dry fully. Roll up a small amount of the putty and smooth it into the chip, being careful to only apply within the chip itself. Leave this to dry overnight. When dry cut a tiny piece of fine grit sandpaper and gently rub the putty. Be careful not to rub any other part of the ceramic as this will scratch it. When this is smooth, use a small artist's brush to paint on a fine layer of acrylic paint that matches your ceramic. When dry, paint on a clear acrylic sealant and leave to dry fully. These repair items can be purchased in a craft shop.

Hornsea Heirloom teacup in Autumn Brown, 1970s

TUPPERWARE

Tupperware revolutionised kitchens and even the way we ate, as food could finally be stored properly thus reducing the need to cook daily. Launched in America in 1946 it took until the 1960s for it to become a kitchen must-have on both sides of the Atlantic. Designed in various colours from pretty pastels to lime green, there is a Tupperware item for all your needs, including cheese graters, jelly moulds, packed lunch boxes, egg cups and of course the basic storage container.

The introduction of the Tupperware Party had a real impact on society. Women had experienced great independence whilst working during the war, which was then given up to return to the kitchen in the 1950s. The role of party hostess provided employment and freedom for women in the comfort and safety of their own home. It was a well-respected job and product. Friends and neighbours were invited over for the evening, to share a glass of sherry and experience the whole range. Excitement ensued, storage items were bought and delivered only days later.

The Harvest range was the most popular in the 1960s, designed in citrus shades from bright yellow to orange. These would contain tea and coffee and be out on display rather than hidden away in the cupboard. It has the classic fanned 'burp'-seal lid, which when fastened ensured your food stayed fresher for longer.

Tupperware Harvest range, c. 1970s

CADDYMATIC

The Caddymatic was a popular plastic tea dispenser that hung on the wall of the 1960s kitchen – a spring-loaded, rocket-shaped device that released the right amount of tea at the press of a button. Made by Arthur Douglas in England they were made in the vibrant kitchen colours of the time, such as orange and bright blue. A space-saving version was designed for smaller homes called the Caddymatic Junior. These have become very collectible over the last few years and would be a great retro addition to your 1960s kitchen.

Caddymatic tea dispenser, c. 1960s

EGG CUPS

The fascination with all things space related influenced the kitchen as well as other areas of the home. Cosmic-shaped plastic egg cups were the choice for brightening up the breakfast table. Often made from melamine, they came in flying saucer shapes with lipped sides for your eggshell. Tupperware made an alternative style with a plastic lid to keep your egg warm, based on the 1930s stainless steel Heatmaster version.

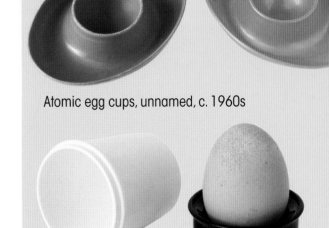

Atomic egg cups, unnamed, c. 1960s

Tupperware egg cups, 1970s

CHICKEN BRICK

Habitat was the store of choice for the baby-boom generation during the late 1960s through to the 1980s. The retailer, owned by Sir Terence Conran, inspired a whole generation with mass-produced, stylish homewares. They often sold items that we had seen on our annual package holiday, redesigning them to fit into UK trends. They were the first to sell the pasta jar, the paper moon lampshade and the duvet, but their bestselling item was the chicken brick.

Made from terracotta, this was an unusual chicken-shaped cooking device embraced by young people setting up home in the 1970s. Its design was simple, its results were impressive. The chicken lay inside the brick and steamed in its own juices like a traditional clay cooking device. The chicken tasted better as it had cooked in a sealed environment. Designed by Queensbury Hunt, it launched in 1968 and it sold in its millions. Recently re-released, sales continue over forty years later.

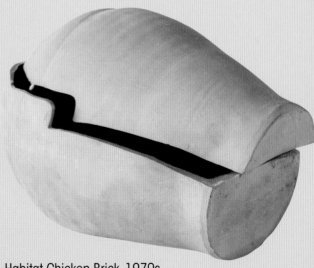

Habitat Chicken Brick, 1970s

Watch Out!
Always place your chicken brick inside a cold oven, so it can warm up gently. This will prevent it from cracking.

CLEANING TIP
Never wash your chicken brick with soap. Soak it in warm water adding a little salt to break down the residue.

NORWEGIAN KITCHENWARE

Scandinavian mid-century design influenced many areas of our homes and is loved for its sleek lines and style. After the war Norway needed to boost its production and economy after years of German occupation, so looked to their interior and product designers to pave the way. This included new modern cookware and tableware. What made them stand out from their neighbours was how they managed to design with both their culture and environment in mind. The end results were stylish pieces in fresh vibrant colours, influenced by the fjords yet still with a folksy feel.

Cathrineholm enamel pots and kettles are no exception and are must-have items in your 1960s kitchen. The company produced stoves from the early 1900s, but it wasn't until they produced the Lotus designs by Grete Prytz Kittelsen that sales really took off. Influenced by American designers in the late 1940s, her vision was a contemporary shape using stainless steel and coloured enamel. The leaf design by Arne Ingemann Clausen was added and the iconic saucepan was born. This included kettles, bowls, even fondue sets in greens, oranges, yellows and blues.

Figgjo Flint also embraced the marriage between contemporary and folk art with their ceramics. Choosing talented young designers and new production methods they created tableware with daisy flowers reminiscent of Cathrineholm's designs, in blues and oranges as well as more traditional scenes, such as the Sago design.

RESTORATION TIP

Remove stubborn burn marks from enamelware with denture cleaner. Fill halfway with warm water and drop in one or two denture tablets and soak until they stop fizzing. This should help to break down some of the stain. Remove the remaining stain by rubbing gently with a scrubbing brush (not a scouring pad as this will scratch).

Catherineholm Lotus kettle and saucepan, 1960s

Flint Sago plaque, 1970s

Catherineholm salt and pepper pots, 1960s

STYLING TIP

These items deserve to be out on display. Stack your Lotus ware on a shelf instead of in a cupboard. Hang your Figgjos on a wall in place of wall art.

LE CREUSET KITCHENWARE

Originating in France in the 1920s, it took until the mid-1970s for the enamel cast-iron cookware to launch globally. In 1972 the Italian designer Enzo Mari came on board and redesigned the traditional ranges with a new, modern look. With the introduction of fondue sets, Le Creuset offered an alternative way to cook, bringing the oven to the table for the first time. Newly married couples impressed their friends with their orange, continental gratin pan with a burner underneath, cooking new dishes, such as veal, in the centre of the table. With the advertising strapline, 'Every good cook should know a little French: Le Creuset', the brand has remained a wedding list must-have forty years on.

CLEANING TIP

Le Creuset pans are dishwasher safe but are best hand washed. Remove food while the pan is still hot and allow to cool before washing. To remove rust from the inside gently rub with a nylon brush, warm water and salt. For stubborn rust use a fine wire wool and hotter water, then wash with washing-up liquid. Line the base of the pan with vegetable oil and place upside down on foil or a tray in a hot oven for an hour. Allow to cool before using/storing.

Le Creuset saucepan, 1970s

STYLING TIP

These brightly coloured cast-iron pans look too good to be put away in the cupboard. Hang from S-shaped hooks on a metal bar on your kitchen wall or from the ceiling on a grid system. Remember these are very heavy pans so make sure all fixings are screwed securely into ceiling joists or wall joists of a stud wall. Mix up multicoloured pans for a bright, pop art effect.

STORAGE JARS

For decades coffee and tea had been stored in metal enamelled canisters. The 1960s introduced the trend of ceramic jars being out on show on your worktop, often in a straight line arranged in size order from a large biscuit jar all the way down to a small sugar jar. Matching bright floral patterns in oranges on a white background were popular, often with wood or cork lids and rubber seals. Transfer-printed styles with handwritten-looking text alluded back to traditional times, but the stylized 1960s flowers always gave their age away. Crown Devon and Taunton Vale introduced matching items, such as flour shakers and butter dishes, enticing us to buy whole sets. The 1970s look was replaced by more sombre brown designs, such as Hornsea's Bronte.

Another popular storage canister was the Kilner jar. Made from glass, this famous preserving jar was designed as early as 1840. It had a glass top sealed by a metal-ridged band that screwed around it. This popular style was re-launched in the 1960s, but with a new plastic surround in red, orange and brown.

STYLING TIP
Arrange your jars on show in a height order line.

RESTORATION TIP
The rubber seals on storage jars can get lost or stretch so the jar isn't airtight. Replacement ones can be easily bought online from sites such as eBay, but make sure you are buying the right seals for the jars you have. If in doubt always ask!

Crown Devon canisters, c. 1960s

STYLING TIP
These jars are great for recreating a pantry feel to your vintage kitchen. Fill them with all your food staples, such as oats and pasta, and display on a convenient, visible shelf. They also look great filled with handpicked flowers for an alternative vintage vase.

Kilner jar with orange screw lid, 1970s

Hornsea Bronte canister, 1970s

CLOCKS

A bright kitchen clock is a must-have for a 1960s/70s kitchen. These were made by Metamec, Smiths and Westclox and were popular in bright colours, such as orange and blue to match your kitchen accessories. With their plain faces, wipeable surface and silver metal fittings, they were designed to be functional compared to the starburst shapes often seen in the lounge.

RESTORATION TIP

Many 1960s kitchen clocks are electric. Convert to a battery operated clock as follows. Gently remove the glass front by removing the screws from the back. Remove the hands and the electric movement. They may be screwed down or glued so use a small knife to ease apart. You will need to buy a battery clock mechanism that fits the hole size, as well as new hands. Slide the battery part in place and tighten the screws supplied. The hands will need to be replaced with the hour hand first and then the minute hand on top. Make sure these are positioned at the 12 o'clock position. The mechanism may need to be glued at the back. Replace the front face and re-screw. Be gentle with this as the glass can break if you apply too much force. Alternatively, use a recommended company to convert your clock for you.

Timemaster clock, West Germany, 1960s

The Finishing Touches:

1. Ceramic chicken ☐
2. Stainless steel teapot ☐
3. Bush radio ☐
4. Beaded curtain over the back door ☐
5. Soda stream ☐

ADELLE SAYS:

Tangerine orange is a favourite colour of ours so we used it as a feature wall in the kitchen. We also have orange highlight pieces throughout this ground floor area, such as the kettle and food mixer. Also, as the kitchen diner is quite open plan to the lounge, we have flashes of orange here too, with artwork, textiles and West German 'fat lava' vases. This helps towards a sense of unity and flow through the whole ground floor of the house.

GET THE LOOK:
Justin and Adelle's kitchen, Todmorden

The large antique baker's table clearly is important here and can provide a valuable working space as well as being a great size to sit all your friends around to enjoy dinner. The Ercol chairs give a rounded shape to contrast with the rectangular table and free-standing butcher's block.

GET THE LOOK:
Heather and
Cleveland's
kitchen, Leeds

The open-plan kitchen diner makes this a sociable space with the white gloss doors lightening up the room. Modern lights, alongside 1970s Hornsea ceramic storage on the windowsill create a contrast that really works.

" HEATHER SAYS:

We are not just really lucky to find the things that we do – we work really hard at it. My partner rarely drives by a charity shop without stopping and popping in. Our favourite thing to do at the weekend is go round local charity shops, or visit a nearby town such as Harrogate, and check out its charity shops. Even when we go on holiday, we look for antiques emporiums or vintage shops: it really is a way of life. "

The dark natural wood worktops mean that splashes of colour, such as the modern ceramic pot, pop out at you. This wood is then echoed in accessories, such as the sphere-shaped salt holder and fruit bowl.

❚❚ HEATHER SAYS:

We add a couple of key colours to each room,
for example teal blue and mustard, and keep
them running through the room. You have to
be quite controlled and not introduce other
colours, or you will lose the sense of harmony.

❚❚

The Living Room

The contemporary look introduced in the 1950s with modern furniture and patterned fabric was still popular through the 1960s and into the 1970s. Matching furniture in glossy teak was the must-have look alongside textured three-piece suites. This was a room for entertaining: couples hosted cocktail parties with drinks served from their homemade bars.

The colours were a little more subdued though, with burnt oranges and dark blues instead of bright yellows and reds. Curtains were still long, but the patterns were more geometric with circles or almost childlike daisy flowers all over in different shades of the same colour. This style was replaced in the 1970s with classic Arts & Crafts prints, such as William Morris's Golden Lily design. Wallpapers were in similar patterns although many chose a simple woodchip and painted over it.

Furniture was curved with round, glass-topped coffee tables and corner sofas that resembled semicircles. This look was influenced by the space-age shapes yet contrasted well with the long horizontal feel of sideboards and wall units.

Cabinets were filled with collections, such as souvenir dolls. With the popularity of package holidays especially to Spain, people would collect a small doll from every country they visited. Other collections, such as ceramic owls, would also be on show. Most homes by the 1970s had high wall units in teak. These were a multipurpose storage system with space for the television, drinks cabinets, a glass-fronted area for displaying ornaments as well as standard cupboards. They impacted the rooms significantly as they were so large and dark.

Floors were carpeted with a long shag pile or a shorter patterned pile made from new man-made fibres. These new materials were very important to entertaining families as they could be easily cleaned. Moroccan-style rugs were popular in psychedelic patterns: they were reversible to give more choice, had tasselled edges and were actually made in the UK.

Fireplaces were filled in with a gas fire with a silver metal grill. Some came with a teak surround made by established and respected furniture manufacturers, such as G Plan. Storage heaters and electric heaters were also popular.

The focal point was the television, with most homes owning one by the end of the 1960s. Alongside the video recorder it quickly became the favourite gadget, with families eating their dinners on trays as they watched evening programmes.

This is an easy look to achieve as most modern furniture retailers have a retro range with sideboards and swivel chairs. However, the originals can also be found at affordable prices online and are often still in good condition. Choose patterned curtains against a cream wall or patterned wallpaper on a feature wall with plain curtains or blinds. Instead of a fitted carpet, choose a 1960s shag-pile rug on stained or painted floorboards for a more modern look. Fill the room with vintage accessories, such as a rocket lamp, art glass and a wall of pictures.

Must-have Items

FURNITURE

Teak furniture from respected manufacturers, such as G Plan, Nathan and McIntosh, became popular in the early 1960s. They designed functional items such as sideboards, giving them a contemporary feel with extra length (some were up to 2m/7ft), integrated handles and a medium gloss finish. Often based on Scandinavian designs desired for their craftsmanship as well as their simple style, families aspired to have matching sets throughout the room. Advertisements sprang up, creating an aspirational world of men drinking cocktails with ladies lounging on day beds. Before this, adverts were about the room set; now they were about the lifestyle. These were popular through the 1970s, with G Plan becoming one of the first UK companies to sell mass-produced furniture. Other woods were also popular: Ercol continued to produce English elm items and rosewood became the wood of choice for higher end pieces.

A modular storage system called Ladderax was designed in 1964, which was a practical yet stylish unit that stood against walls. Designed by Robert Heal for Staples of Cricklewood, UK, it was loved for its versatility and the fact that it was self-supporting with no wall fixings needed. The system consisted of teak shelves, cupboards, drawers and pull-down cocktail units, which could be positioned exactly as you wanted. Each section was bookmarked by a pair of black or white metal ladder-type ends, which gave the effect that each part was almost floating on the wall. Other companies designed their own more affordable versions, such as Avalon. Ladderax were made until the 1980s and are about to re-launch a new version for the 21st century.

This modern style, however, wasn't to everyone's taste. The baby-boom generation, leaving the family home in the late 1960s rejected this 'contemporary furniture'. They saved up for one key piece, such as a Sanderson sofa with William Morris fabric or a Habitat chrome glass side table. Interestingly they also inherited their grandparents utility furniture and up-cycled it to give it a fresh, modern look. Tables were painted in black or white gloss, proving that these designs had passed the test of time.

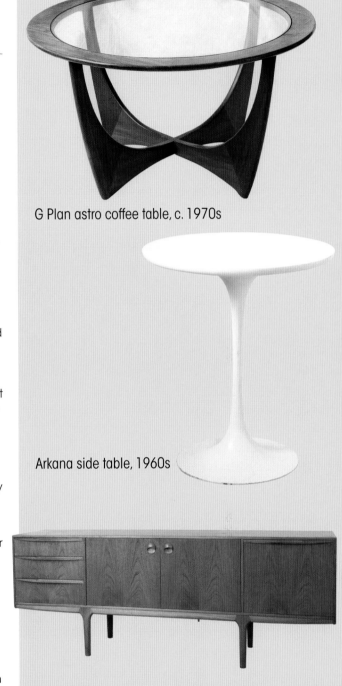

G Plan astro coffee table, c. 1970s

Arkana side table, 1960s

McIntosh sideboard, c. 1970s

RESTORATION TIP

Hide scratches on teak by using a gentle dab of scratch cover applied with a soft duster. Medium wood finish is best for classic teak, but test a patch underneath before you start. For more stubborn marks, gently sand the teak then apply teak oil sparingly. Be careful though, as this won't work on teak veneer.

The more design-led homes were filled with space-influenced styles, such as the white tulip-based table and chairs. First designed by Finland's Eero Saarinen in 1956, it was then copied by Maurice Burke for Arkana in the 1960s. It came with small stools and side tables to create a total cosmic look. Denmark's Arne Jacobsen designed the egg chair in 1958, which influenced reclining chairs throughout the next two decades. With its swivel mechanism, winged back and gentle rocking action, this style was reproduced over again in vinyl or the later velveteen material well into the early 1980s. Maybe the piece with the most humour is the hanging cane chair. For students and young couples alike it was the perfect home accessory, especially for a party. With its heavy chain attached to the ceiling, it literally hung in the corner often with a sheepskin rug inside. This look was considered fun and fresh, complementing the shapes of the lighting and glassware of the time, compared to the serious matching suites belonging to the older generation.

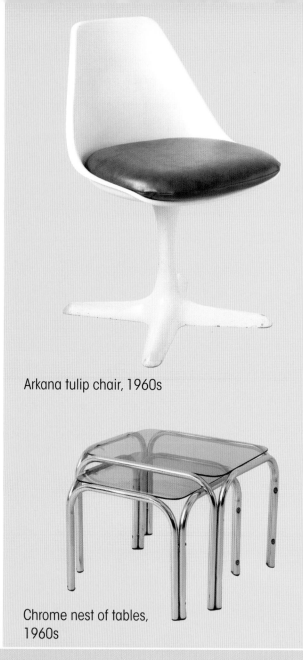

Arkana tulip chair, 1960s

CLEANING TIP

Chrome can attract surface rust spots, but these can easily be removed especially if you attend to it early. First clean the area with a wet cloth and then pat dry. Put some chrome polish onto the rust and also onto a piece of fine steel wool. Rub the rust patch with the steel wool without too much force so you don't scratch it. Add more polish if needed. After a few minutes the rust should be gone. If it's still there it means the rust is on the deeper metal underneath the chrome finish, which alas cannot be removed. Lastly, polish the chrome with a soft cloth.

Chrome nest of tables, 1960s

STYLING TIP

Teak furniture looks great in a modern home with its clean lines and simplicity. With a plain wall and a stained wooden floor, a 1960s sideboard or coffee table will look as contemporary now as it did then.

LIGHTING

Lighting during this period was heavily influenced by our love affair with all things cosmic. At a time when the Victorian reproduction look was booming, spaceship-like shades emerged with interwoven pieces made from gently folded plastic or metal. Furniture designers of the time also got on board with Guzzini's pull-down mushroom light and Panton's astronaut helmet-inspired lamp. For budgets that couldn't stretch to these, the choice was a simple paper moon shade. Habitat in the UK introduced these in the 1960s and it quickly became one of their bestselling lines.

The defining lights of this era were both rocket shaped. The lava lamp was designed in 1963, but didn't become popular until later in the decade. The hippy generation loved its psychedelic feel, but with its torpedo shape and flowing lava inside, it is reminiscent of outer space. The rocket lamp made from spun resin was a must-have in the 1960s. Standing on three teak legs, the orange rocket is tall and eye-catching, and when lit up sends a warm glow around the room.

A 1970s classic is the ceramic lava lamp with its elongated woven shade. Often with two bulbs, the holes around it ensured light literally flooded out from all angles.

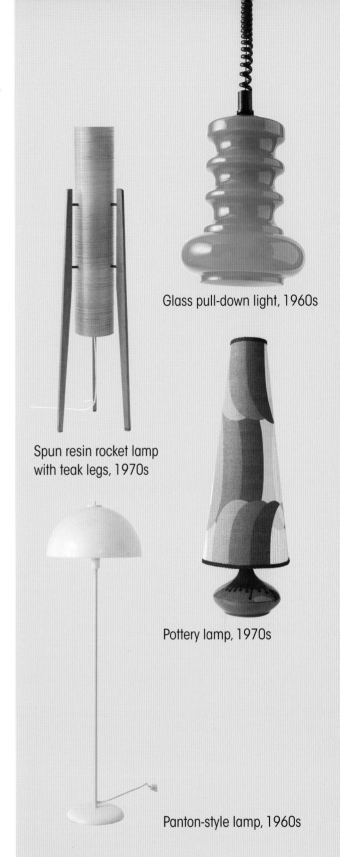

Glass pull-down light, 1960s

Spun resin rocket lamp with teak legs, 1970s

Pottery lamp, 1970s

Panton-style lamp, 1960s

Watch Out!
Vintage lights up until the 1980s will probably not have modern wiring. Where possible you should buy a PAT (Portable Appliance Tested) light, but if you are in doubt get your retro lights checked by a qualified electrician.

G·LASS

It took until the 1960s for us to fully buy into a new funky look in glassware. Italian glass with its fluid-cased creations, Scandinavian glass with its retro styling and American cylindrical-shaped bottles all brightened up our teak sideboards and are still collectible today.

The cased Murano form from Italy was developed as early as 1934. It has a clear glass casing that houses a brightly coloured shape within it, creating a beautiful layered effect. Adding extra colours into the mix means that when the sun shines through it, different colours are seen to be reflected. The most famous and desirable was the Sommerso range. Popular in the 1960s, these styles influenced American and Czech art glass, which is more affordable today.

In Scandinavia, manufacturers, such as Holmegaard and Riihimäki created modern, affordable and fun shapes that really sum up the design style of the 1960s. These pieces were mass-produced for the first time and are still very desirable today. Unusually, it was three talented women who were behind the interesting shapes at Riihimäki, designing great stand-alone vases with new textures and angular cylindrical shapes.

Blenko designed tall, elegant decanters in America in bold, striking colours. Starting his career making stained glass, he moved onto these geometric, sometimes textured bottles in the late 1950s influencing the European glass manufacturers two decades later. Retro medicine bottles from Italy and France were popular well into the 1970s, but were now in the more muted tones of the decade.

Holmegaard vase, c. 1960s

Murano freeform glass, c. 1960s

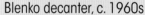

Blenko decanter, c. 1960s

STYLING TIP

Don't be afraid to group multiple vases and bowls together to create maximum impact on a windowsill or sideboard. Choose a central piece and add contrasting shapes and colours either side in a symmetrical way. Select three key colours and alternate within the group.

CLOCKS

The British clock maker Metamec led the way in the 1960s with their starburst and sunray wall-hung clocks. Most modern homes had one adorning their walls, as they were designed to complement any style. These ranged from classic teak to a glossy gold metal – whether your home was modern or traditional there would be a look for you.

The 1970s wall clock was large faced often with a pine surround. Like many 1970s trends these clocks looked to the past with their Roman numerals yet with their now modern battery mechanism.

RUGS

No home in the 1970s was without a shag-pile carpet or rug. Wool rugs in 1970s autumnal muted tones added texture and softness to a room, with some people even hanging them on the wall. The look originated from Sweden, which produced patterned long pile, hand-knotted ryas (rya means rug) often used as bedding. The UK made their version with Scandinavian sounding names, such as the Finlandia rya rug. Alongside teak or chrome they now look brilliant on stripped floorboards in a modern vintage home.

Homes that couldn't stretch to a rya turned to the craft of rug making. Making rag rugs had been popular since the 1930s, peaking in the latter half of the 1970s. All that was needed were strips of old material, a knitting needle and burlap (the jute-like backing). Clubs formed and books were written to encourage women to make their own patterned floor coverings. Keeping them in tip top form was important for the 1970s homeowner with continuous care to ensure each fibre was standing proud.

Axminster Finlandia rug, 1960s

STYLING TIP

Group three starburst clocks on a feature wall, such as at the end of a corridor on your landing. Make sure you set them for the same time so as not to confuse. Alternatively, set them for three different time zones.

Metamec starburst clock, c. 1970s

Pine clock, 1970s

CLEANING TIP

Shake your rug firmly outside or hang it over a washing line and then use a vintage carpet beater to get all the crumbs and dust out of the thick pile. Invest in a plastic rake (try a children's toy one) to literally comb the fibres of your rug before your guests arrive (and after)!

WALL ART

In the 1960s, for the first time, prints were mass-produced on the high street. Boots in the UK and Turner Manufacturing in Chicago, turned unknown artists into household names with millions of us buying identical pictures. Two of the most popular were J.H. Lynch and Tretchikoff, who painted strong women in vivid colours. Lynch's *Tina* is the most famous of all with her sultry eyes becoming the thing of dreams for most 1960's boys!

Alternatives were classic Impressionist and Surrealist prints, such as Manet's *Le dejeuner sur l'herbe* and Van Gogh's *Starry night*, reproduced onto a heavy backboard.

The 1970's love of the Arts & Crafts movement resulted in reproduction advertisements by Mucha and Toulouse-Lautrec gracing our walls. Originating from the late 1800s, these styles were hugely popular, with their muted tones complementing the fabrics of William Morris.

These images were often on mirrors. With crude wooden frames, classic images such as Moët & Chandon became popular. Interior designers also embraced this trend with Ringo Star's company, Ringo and Robin, creating Warhol-type images on glass. Abstract wire creations were also popular, with metallic threads woven around nails to form geometric designs, such as boats.

J.H. Lynch's *Tina*, 1960s

Mucha reproduction print *Autumn*, 1970s

Tretchikoff *The Chinese Girl*, 1960s

STYLING TIP

Create a wall of framed prints on a feature wall. Be careful not to choose too many eye-catching, iconic prints within the same grouping as this will overpower the effect. For best results use different sizes, textures and frames within the same grouping to avoid the end result becoming too symmetrical.

WEST GERMAN POTTERY

The Bauhaus movement in the 1920s celebrated great modern art, including sculpture and pottery. With all factories closing down during World War II, it took until the 1950s for these artists to continue with the work they had started decades earlier. By the 1960s they were producing pottery from many factories, including Scheurich, Jopeko and Roth. By now the designs were more extravagant with bright colours, fluid shapes and textured lava surfaces.

The base colours were often in earthy tones, with bright oranges, greens and blues layered on top in a shiny glaze. In a time of hope after years of oppression, the forms represented the optimism towards the future. The layers of lava however represent the concerns of the artists: the development of nuclear weapons and the cold war were threatening their optimism.

The factories closed down in the 1970s, but their legacy continues in collections around the world. They are loved for their abstract strength, for the strength in the design, the strength that they represent and the strength of the artist who came back to show the world that German design was as strong as ever.

STYLING TIP

Group smaller pieces in large clusters, or on windowsills or sideboards. Select your colour choice then mix it up with different shapes and finishes. Highly glazed vases look great beside matt ones to really emphasize their shine. Try collecting items with a similar theme, for example, side handles that can be repeated throughout the group. Large pieces, such as stand-alone vases, look better sitting on the floor.

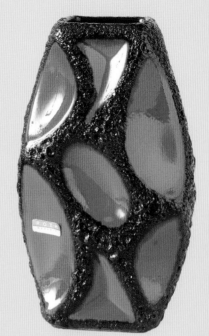

Roth vase, 1970s

Scheurich pitcher, 1970s

The Finishing Touches:

1. Flower curtains and cushions ☐
2. Houseplants ☐
3. Leather footstool ☐
4. Teak deer ornaments ☐
5. Teak radiogram ☐

GET THE LOOK: Justin and Adelle's living room, Todmorden

Hanging a variety of prints on the wall in different shapes and sizes adds real interest to the far wall. Your eyes are drawn there but then pulled back to the large print above the sofa. Even though they are from different eras, Justin and Adelle have cleverly mixed antiques with retro styles, creating an inviting and interesting home.

" ADELLE SAYS:

We like to live with a mix of vintage, mid-century modern and much older country antiques. With a bit of thought they can sit quite happily with each other – artwork, ceramics and textiles tie it all together. Favourites of ours are 20th century Northern Industrial artists, which work well. The wood burning stove is a focal point in the lounge and it allows you to heat the room you're in without having to put the central heating on in the rest of the house. An alcove filled with logs is very attractive as well as being practical. "

GET THE LOOK: Heather and Cleveland's living room, Leeds

Heather has re-upholstered the occasional chair in patterned fabric with an African feel to complement the artefacts out on display. Her handmade cushions add a soft touch to the clean lines of the furniture and the neutral tones of the room create a calming influence.

HEATHER SAYS:

We like to create interest by putting three-dimensional things on the walls, such as antlers, bowls and masks. This stops everything from looking too flat.

The Hall

Before the 1960s the hall was just the place where you hung your coat and took the odd telephone call. As phones were becoming more accessible and affordable, families now sat in the hallway to chat the evening away to their friends.

To make their calls they sat on telephone seats or simply on the bottom step of the stairs. The newly invented teenager in particular took this hall space as their own to arrange their social calendar.

Fast forward fifty years and the hallway has again become redundant; with the invention of cordless and mobile phones there is no need to sit here anymore. Why not re-juvenate this space by creating a picture gallery on one wall or displaying a retro phone on a small teak cupboard? Make it a space to welcome you home rather than an empty corridor.

Trimphone, c. 1970s

BT 700 series, 1960s–80s

Princess phone, 1960s

RESTORATION TIP

Retro telephones should still work in a modern socket, but make sure you test them before you buy. They will not work with call centres however, as they don't have the same keypad facilities that a modern phone has. They can be converted, but it's best to hire a professional company.

Must-have Items

TELEPHONES

Up until now a telephone was something you hired from the General Post Office (GPO), which was the forerunner to British Telecom (BT). The telephone was for adults and most homes didn't even have one. The arrival of the BT 700 series in the 1960s changed the face of our communication as well as brightening up our teak telephone tables. These were called the 'modern telephone' and were available in seven colours. Only a third of us were brave enough to have a coloured version though, the most popular colours still being black or cream. BT introduced the idea of swapping colours to bring a change to your decor, but as this cost money most parents chose a safe, neutral colour.

The Trimphone was introduced in the UK in the late 1960s and was famous for its ringtone, which was more of a warble than a ring. With its lit-up dial and volume control this phone was a cool alternative to the basic styles that came before.

In America, the Princess phone was designed as a bedroom phone as this also lit up. In pretty colours such as pastel pink it was clearly aimed at women, as the name suggests. Phones were now seen as a home accessory to match your decor and paved the way for the many fun styles that were to come in the 1980s.

TELEPHONE TABLES

No 1960s home was without a telephone table. Made from teak these were slimline so they could fit into small spaces. Often with vinyl seat pads, the idea was that you had somewhere to sit while chatting to your friends. Before this time the telephone was for calling the doctor or for other emergencies, but with the dawn of the teenager it had become an essential home accessory. The design was sleek and practical, with drawers for your phone book. Telephone shelves were introduced for homes with the tiniest of halls so your new coloured phone could still sit in pride of place in your hall.

STYLING TIP

If you have space, choose a teak unit with glass doors. This gives you a great space to display your retro telephones if you don't want them out on show in every room.

Myer telephone table, 1960s

COAT STANDS

Putting your coats on the newel post simply wasn't good enough in your 1960s hallway. Many homes had a teak wall-hung system with a top shelf, coat hooks and even a small storage cupboard at the base. Its neat, compact and practical nature made this ideal for small spaces.

The molecular structured ball feet popular in the 1950s continued well into this decade, appearing on hooks and coat stands. Hago made black metal stands with bright plastic teardrop-shaped tips, with an extra space for your vintage brollies. Based on the traditional wood styles, this gave homes a young, fresh feel.

The Italian company Kartell introduced furniture made from plastic in the 1960s. With a glossy finish, they brought in established designers to create clever, often modular storage perfect for bedrooms, offices and kids rooms. They also designed a great white plastic coat stand. With hooks pointing in all directions, it has been copied ever since.

Yellow Hago coat stand, 1960s

The Finishing Touches:

1. *Teak plant stand* ☐
2. *Floor-standing ceramic pot for brollies* ☐
3. *Ball feet letter rack* ☐
4. *Teak-framed mirror* ☐
5. *Starburst barometer* ☐

GET THE LOOK:
Our hall, Cranfield, Bedfordshire

We reintroduced classic bannisters to create a light and airy hallway, giving a sense of space. This traditional look contrasts with the 1960s splayed-leg, teak display cabinet, where we display our vintage phone collection. We have chosen a simple colour scheme to run through; the mint green of the Ericofon and the horse print is a calming shade and perfect to return to after a hard day.

The Dining Room

Dining rooms in the 1960s were joined onto the living room in an open-plan style. This created a more social space perfect for the new craze of hosting dinner parties. During the recession of the 1970s, couples stayed in rather than going out in the evening and invited their friends to join them.

They cooked foreign cuisine that they had eaten on their annual holiday, such as spaghetti bolognese or mushroom stroganoff. Celebrity chefs were appearing on the television and inspired couples were desperate to show off their culinary skills as well as their homes. Dinner would be served on matching plates, which were bought for them as wedding presents, alongside stainless steel cutlery, which was stored in a teak canteen with an orange velvet-feel lining.

The dining table and sideboard were coordinated in teak or rosewood and in similar styles to the living room. Tables were designed with extra leaves inside so they could be extended to accommodate extra guests. The table was laid meticulously, often with fabric placemats and coasters.

A heated serving plate was placed in the centre of the table to keep your food warm while you served yourself. However, the hostess would often serve you directly through the kitchen hatch, first seen in the 1950s home. Another option was to wheel the food in on a heated hostess trolley. These were cumbersome items made from a teak veneer. The lid on top came off to reveal serving dishes in stainless steel. On the side was a pull-down door with a grill pan inside. With the advertising slogan, 'The Hostess with the Mostest', the hotplate created some theatre at the table while flaming liqueur on your crêpe suzettes.

Just like the living room, it is easy to find retro-style dining furniture from modern retailers. However, originals can be bought at affordable prices, especially dining tables and chairs by G Plan. Choose vintage wallpaper for a feature wall or select a great reproduction version, such as Orla Kiely's range for Harlequin. Once you have decorated and accessorized your room, why not host your own 1970s dinner party with retro food and styling?

Must-have Items

STAINLESS STEEL

Old Hall stainless steel was a popular wedding present in the 1960s and would be used to impress your guests on your G Plan dining table. Young couples preferred this to the traditional china dinner service used by their parents.

The respected designer Robert Welch joined forces with the company in the 1950s having studied in Sweden. Scandinavian design clearly influenced his style, with its clean lines and practicality. The most stylish and award-winning range was called Alveston, which took a modern twist on traditional styles. The teapot reminded people of the genie's lamp, resulting in the alternative name of Aladdin. The Minister of State for Technology even took a tea set and cutlery canteen as gifts to Russia in 1967 to highlight the UK's great craftsmanship. The most commercial range was called Connaught and can be easily found today.

TABLE CENTREPIECES

How you laid your table in the 1960s/70s was nearly as important as the food you served. The centrepiece needed to be eye-catching yet elegant. Candles had been functional items until now, used as a replacement for electric light. Stainless steel Old Hall candlesticks were popular to coordinate with your tableware. In the 1970s a candle was often placed in an empty bottle of Mateus Rosé wine, reminding couples of their holidays. Another popular choice was the atomic bubbly table decoration, which was inspired by the molecular structures seen in the 1950s. These were available in various colours and were the choice for the hippy generation.

CLEANING TIP
Always wash and dry stainless steel by gently rubbing in the direction of the grain using a non-abrasive cloth. Stainless steel can appear dull after use so get extra shine by rubbing with all-purpose flour and a soft cloth. Alternatively, rub in a few drops of baby oil.

Old Hall salt and pepper pots, 1960s

Old Hall Alveston teapot, 1962

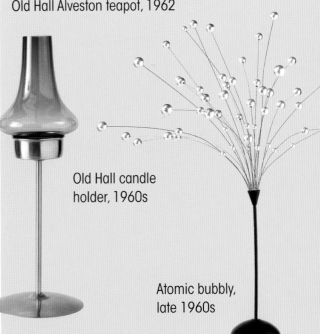

Old Hall candle holder, 1960s

Atomic bubbly, late 1960s

CLEANING TIP
Remove spilt wax from your table by freezing it. Place a few ice cubes in a freezer bag and leave on the wax for fifteen minutes. When it is rock hard, gently scrape using a plastic spatula, being careful not to scratch the table surface.

BULLS

The love affair with Spanish holidays influenced not only our cuisine, but also the plates we ate from. Beefeater plates with large, colourful bulls were the perfect size and shape for your sirloin steak.

Ceramic studio pottery bulls adorned our sideboards with colourful glazes in blues and reds. The best example is the Bitossi bull designed in Italy in the early 1960s. Its high glaze, textured surface and large size (30cm/12in long), makes this is a real collectable. For a British and more affordable version choose the Lotus bull with its daisy pattern on the side.

Beefeater plates, c. 1970s

Lotus ceramic bull, c. 1960s

FONDUE

Fondue parties were hugely popular in the 1970s, where groups of friends met and shared melted cheese from the same pot.

Originating from Switzerland the word fondue means 'to melt', and here in this table top heated pan, multiple cheeses melted together. Long forks with teak handles were used to dip bread into the mixture. Traditions state that a man who drops his bread in the cheese must buy everyone a drink. If a lady does the same she must kiss the people to the side of her. Who needs party games when you've got a fondue set?

CLEANING TIP

Never put teak utensils in the dishwasher. Wash with warm soapy water and dry immediately. To protect the teak, rub in a small amount of mineral oil and leave for 30 minutes. Rub off any excess oil with a soft cloth. Do not use for a few days after oil is applied.

Fondue set, 1970s

FURNITURE

The dining table of choice in the 1960s was the G Plan Fresco range. Made from teak veneer with afromosia detailing, this range consisted of a table with vinyl-seat padded chairs and a matching sideboard.

In here the best stainless steel cutlery and dinner service would be kept for easy table laying. This grown-up range was often purchased at a department store on credit, as keeping up with the Jones's was highly important for the new dinner party pastime.

On return from the annual package holiday to Spain, Father would recreate in the corner of the room the bar he drank from. The hula theme from the 1950s was gone and replaced with a teak bar, along with macramé hanging baskets, punch bowls for sangria and nibbles bowls for your peanuts and olives.

CLEANING TIP

To remove fresh water marks on your teak you need to act fast. As the liquid has only penetrated the top layer you will need to quickly get an iron and a white cotton towel or T-shirt. Turn the iron to its lowest setting and ensure there is no steam action or water inside. Cover the mark with the towel and apply the iron for a few seconds only on top of the towel. Check to see if the mark has dried out. If not, repeat until the mark is dry.

Elliotts of Newbury dining suite, 1960s

Danish Lazy Susan nibbles bowls, c. 1960s

STYLING TIP

Coloured plastic deer were mass-produced at this time to replicate the Babycham deer. These make great place cards with your guests' names on and will definitely bring a smile to your diners' faces!

The Finishing Touches:

1. A bottle of Blue Nun wine ☐
2. Heated plate warmer ☐
3. Punch bowl and glasses ☐
4. Woven placemats ☐
5. After-dinner party games ☐

GET THE LOOK: Heather and Cleveland's dining room, Leeds

Heather and Cleveland have an amazing dining table as it swivels round to become a coffee table. This means that this space is multi-functional: they can start the evening eating dinner, then finish off creating more of a living room.

" HEATHER SAYS:

There are some key components to our style of decor. Natural elements: lots of wood, stone, marble, metals (bronze, copper, gold), bone, horn, antlers, hide and fur. This is a Scandinavian influence and it adds a sense of comfort and calm, but also texture and tactility. We are big fans of vintage African art and sculpture, and that ties in with 1950s and 60s style because it has a connection with, and an influence on jazz music and art. But also, Africana adds an edge, a bit of voodoo, a bit of the dark side, a bit of molasses in the mix. "

GET THE LOOK:
Our bedroom, Cranfield, Bedfordshire

Our bedroom is a mixture of 1950s and 1960s: classic kidney shapes mixed with later atomic shapes. The Poole Pottery ceramic urn sitting on the floor belonged to my grandmother and the white Dresden rabbits on the cabinet belonged to my mum: the room is a mix of recent finds and sentimental pieces, which makes me sleep happily at night!

We found a piece of 1950s Sanderson wallpaper lining a drawer in a chest we bought. Amazingly, it was the same pattern as the reproduction wall paper we have on the feature wall behind our bed. We framed it to hang proudly alongside each other.

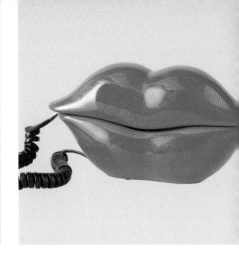

1980s–1990s

The 1980s were a time of contrast, moving from recession in 1982 to the biggest boom our world has ever experienced and then back to bust in 1987. Margaret Thatcher and Ronald Reagan were in charge of the UK and US respectively, making it a totally different place from the decade before. In the UK, businesses were privatized, council houses were bought by their tenants and the yuppie was born. This 'young urban professional' spent money on homes, holidays, clothes and food, creating an almost hedonistic climate. They craved anything 'designer' and bought into new technology. The baby-boomers were grown up and could now buy things their parents had only dreamt of. Tom Wolfe described them as the 'splurge generation' with their fast cars and even faster spending habits.

The design of electronic gadgets developed at a quickening pace during this time. The home computer from Amstrad and Commodore launched in 1981, Windows in 1985 and the biggest development of all, the World Wide Web was invented in 1989. By the early 1990s we had access to almost infinite knowledge at the click of a mouse, which opened our eyes wider than ever before. The mobile phone launched and quickly became the must-have accessory for the yuppie generation.

The rich bought fine art, while the rest of us bought Impressionist prints from Athena. We collected anything from video games to Smurfs. Our homes were decorated in pastel colours with floral, frilled accessories; furniture was black, chrome and flat-packed.

However, all this ended in 1987 on Black Monday when the global stock market crashed. Reminiscent of the Wall Street Crash in America almost 60 years earlier, its effect was the largest since the Great Depression, lasting well into the 1990s.

The rest of the world was evolving fast. China's manufacturing powers were growing, with UK businesses moving their production there. The Soviet Union relations with the US were improving and in 1989 communist Eastern Europe was opened up with the demise of the Berlin Wall.

The recession in the early 1990s made us look to the past as we embraced the late 1960s hippy vibe, decorating our homes with crystals and sunflowers. We were concerned about nuclear threat, marched for the Campaign for Nuclear Disarmament (CND) and travelled further afield discovering new cultures. As in the 1960s we brought back souvenirs to adorn our homes, such as African sculptures, Moroccan rugs and Indian throws to hide our 1980s sofas.

Some don't consider the 1980s and early 1990s as vintage, but many items from this time are becoming collectable. The bright, iconic pieces are being bought by the younger generation as well as people wanting to reminisce. This look works really well with the 1960s style. Andy Warhol, popular in the 1960s, died in 1987, kick-starting a love of pop art and its comic-book style. Use these bright visuals as a starting point, teaming them with retro glass and lighting alongside some of the must-haves on the following pages. This is a fun look with a cartoonlike humour, so it's best not to take it too seriously!

The Kitchen

Kitchen design was still predominantly white throughout the decade, with integrated metal handles running alongside the top of each door. However, with the boom of branded goods, kitchens would be filled with accessories with the family's favourite logos on. Tinware, clocks and milk bottles adorned shelves and walls. A small table would be used for breakfast in the corner with primary-coloured metal chairs from stores like Habitat. Many families chose a chair in each colour to create a bit of fun and to contrast with the sometimes drab kitchen cabinets.

An alternative look was the 'country cottage' style of heavy wooden doors with ornate cornices. An open-shelved curved end would be the place to display your ceramics, while saucepans would hang from the ceiling.

The microwave oven was the must-have appliance; at this time it was very big with a dark finish, often brown. Housewives saved their money for months, as these appliances weren't cheap, and by 1986 approximately a quarter of homes owned one.

Must-have Items

STORAGE

In the late 1970s tins became popular, replacing the earlier trend for ceramic kitchen storage. Replicas of antique advertisement tins sold in their millions and paved the way for a tinware boom in the 1980s and early 1990s. Suddenly all kitchen staples from biscuits to sugar were stored in tins that resembled the packaging you had just thrown away. Orange Jacob's Cream Crackers, red Digestive biscuits and green PG Tips tins were all proudly displayed to create a bright worktop. Like plastic Tupperware decades earlier, all types of storage were available, such as pencil boxes, packed lunch boxes and jewellery boxes.

If metal wasn't your thing then glass storage jars were the choice. They resembled the ceramic jars from the 1960s, but were now more streamlined in shape with geometric patterns all over. White glass with red writing and lid, brown/black glass with cream writing and lid with one thing in common – no flowers! With the increased popularity in travel influencing our culinary tastes the pasta jar became a must-have item in your kitchen.

Jacob's Cream Crackers tin by Armstrong and Clayden, Bedford, 1980s

Glass kitchen canisters, 1980s

Mary Quant charity tin by Armstrong and Clayden, Bedford, 1986

STYLING TIP

Vintage tins look great in a child's room and make excellent storage for their chalks, pens, crafting bits and hair bobbles. Display them on shelves so their bright colours fit right in with the modern vintage playroom feel.

ADVERTISING MILK BOTTLES

In 1981, the UK milk manufacturers introduced colourful advertising on milk bottles. As supermarkets were growing in popularity, independent milk companies needed to generate revenue in innovative ways. Advertising established brands was a winning strategy and continued well into the 1990s. With transfers highlighting breakfast brands, such as Kellogg's cereal, Maxwell House coffee and even Colgate toothpaste, they created a bright, fun way to start your day.

STYLING TIP
These milk bottles look great on display on a visible shelf in your kitchen. Use them as vases for single flower stems from your garden in the middle of your kitchen table. A vintage milk bottle crate will add to the look as well as keeping them safe from harm!

RESTORATION TIP
Remove old water marks from milk bottles by pouring in warm water with two dissolved denture tablets and leaving for half an hour. Rinse out fully and then remove any stubborn marks by gently scrubbing with a baby bottle brush.

ALESSI KITCHENWARE

The Italian company Alessi designed great metal kitchenware that became iconic in the late 1980s/early 1990s. Established in 1921 from a village famous for its metal and wood craft, the company took on established designers to really push the brand forward.

In 1985, Michael Graves designed the kettle with a bird at the spout that whistles when the water has boiled. This design was a real turning point for Alessi, heralding the start of mass production. Based on an Art Deco style with its highly polished finish and triangular shape, it is often considered the best looking kettle ever designed.

Phillip Stark's Juicy Salif, a silver metal juicer standing on three elongated legs, became a signature piece for the company and is still made today. The design classic is also practical as the juice can easily be collected underneath. Another firm favourite is the Anna G corkscrew designed by Alessandro Mendini in 1994. In the shape of a woman, the design has gone on to form part of an extended range of gadgets, such as the kitchen timer. Alessi's range is practical, tongue-in-cheek and without doubt has passed the test of time.

Unigate advertising milk bottles, late 1980s

Alessi kettle, juicer and pan stand, 1980s–1990s

Watch Out!
These items are not dishwasher proof! Simply rinse in warm soapy water and dry immediately.

The Living Room

The living room had two looks in the 1980s – pretty pastels or stylish black with chrome. The pastel look was often peach with patterned, puffed sofas and ornate pelmet curtains. Stencilling was the craze of the moment, with florals and crests painted around the cornice of the room. The alternative look was black ash laminate. This was flat packed, with families learning to assemble their bookcases and tables for the first time. Teamed with glass tables with shiny chrome legs, large directional spotlights and leather sofas, it was an updated version of the 1960s look. Suddenly furniture showrooms sprang up, enticing families to update their 1970s style to a more glamorous look, often on credit.

Another trend was for red, grey and white with touches of black. Wallpaper was either heavily floral or with abstract dashes all over. Flooring was carpeted in a soft pile; it would take until the 1990s for wooden laminate to become the first choice.

In the 1990s, we started to use more industrial finishes and textures in our homes, such as concrete and stainless steel, although many homes chose new exotic woods, reminiscent of those seen on their travels to the Far East. Indian mirrored throws, wall hangings, sunflower book ends and mobiles with moons and stars on were popular.

Must-have Items

SWATCH CLOCK

In 1983, a revolution in watches hit our high streets called Swatch. Designed to be your second watch, they were plastic, colourful and affordable. They quickly became a must-have fashion accessory, with people wearing three at a time or even popping the faces out to wear as badges.

Swatch soon designed other products to build on their successful brand, such as hair watches, telephones and the giant wall clock. At a staggering 210cm (83in) the Swatch wall clock was certainly eye-catching. With its bright colour, Swiss mechanism and fun style it was a must for a teenage bedroom in the early 1990s.

WALL ART

The 1980s were the decade of the poster. Athena led the way with their mass-produced art that graced the walls of everyone from teenagers to students, as well as framed versions for their parents. Their iconic tennis player print in 1977 sold in its millions, but the poster retailer struggled to follow its success until years later. In the early 1980s a new range was designed aimed at teenage girls. The Kiss series by Syd Brak depicted images that inspired young girls to dream of their future, with images of love, kissing and the angst of lost love. The air-brushed neon images with their white-out faces were replicated in fashion on oversized T-shirts and on album covers.

Patrick Nagel, a US artist, designed 1980s pin-ups with an Art Deco feel to them. Most famous for Duran Duran's *Rio* album cover, he created images of women with angular black hair and the classic 1980s white-out faces. With bright colours contrasting against the womens' skin, these posters are now highly collectable. Nagel died in 1984 aged 38, leaving behind a bright future.

The Pop Art of the 1960s had a resurgence in the late 1980s due to the unexpected death of Andy Warhol in 1987. The cartoon-like images of Andy Warhol and Roy Lichtenstein summed up the fun, tongue-in-cheek design of the decade with its bright colours and comic book-style graphics. Into the 1990s our art prints became more serious, with the bold squares of Mark Rothko heralding the start of the minimalist style.

Swatch Floral Story clock, 1993

ONE WAY

NO ENTRY

Athena prints, 1980s

TELEPHONES

Phones in the 1980s were fun! Like many other homewares from this decade the look for telephones was quirky, brightly-coloured and geometric.

The Genie phone was designed to be glamorous, with its curved oval shape and circular push buttons in the style of a rotary dial. The advert showed a lady in her bedroom in a silky negligee using the Genie. Described as adding, 'an element of sophistication to any interior' and 'that final touch of class to any room setting' it was even made in the popular decorating colour of the early 1980s – peach.

Novelty phones were not just for kids. Whereas the Mickey Mouse and Snoopy phone were clearly aimed at children, the pouting red lips phone was great for her, and the hamburger or the flash car was perfect for him. If this was a little too much for you, then the clear phone, which revealed the inner workings and lit up when someone called, was the one. Swatch made a Twinphone with two phones in one so you could have a three-way conversation. Marketed as being 'phone-tastic', this was popular well into the 1990s.

Another key look was a modern version of old phones. The Empress was designed to look like an antique phone and came in floral patterns, while the Candlestick looked like a 1920s phone in glossy white or black. Interestingly, they were also advertised with a lady wearing silk and lace in her bedroom.

BT Genie phone, 1980s

Lips phone, 1980s

Swatch Twinphone, 1990s

Mickey Mouse phone, 1990s

BT Empress and Candlestick phones, 1980s

GET THE LOOK: Sarah G.'s home, Bedfordshire

The bright primary colours of the 1980s homewares look great alongside the 1960s pop look. Both looks are fun, resulting in a home that has interest at every point. Offset against the neutral tones of the kitchen doors, walls and sofa, this look simply brings a smile to my face. Particular favourites are the Snowdon designed Trimphone, the tuxedo print with a slight deco feel and the giant Swatch wall clock.

SARAH SAYS:

I love the fun, cheeky vibe of the 80s mixed with the modernist style of the 60s. Bright colours make me feel happy and elements of quirky design, such as Alessi kitchenware, make me not take the design of my home too seriously. My home is incredibly important to me – it must look right but also feel happy, warm, inviting and fun.

Further Rooms

Any room in the house, or garden for that matter, can receive the vintage treatment and here I suggest ways in which you can develop your eye and passion for the vintage look and bring the style to any area that you live, work and play in, including children's rooms, studies and gardens.

All rooms have the possibility to be styled with vintage. A baby's nursery with bunting made from vintage fabric, old rag dolls and a handmade crochet blanket will create a space filled with a sense of innocence and nostalgia. A boy's room decorated with 1970s Superhero wallpaper and metal Tonka trucks will make him the envy of all his friends. And what could be prettier than a little girl's room filled with 1960s dolls, vintage tea sets and framed school prints on the wall?

Working from home would be great in a home office filled with 1980s orange plastic filing drawers and a retro telephone. Afterwards, you can relax in the garden on a striped deck chair, sitting by herbs and flowers planted in 1940s ceramic sinks and enamel watering cans.

In this final section, the must-have items and styling tips will inspire you to get the look throughout your home and fill your life with all things vintage.

The Children's Room

Children today live in a battery-operated world. In years gone by, they played with wood or metal toys passed down through the generations, lovingly worn from years of play. Families came together to play board games rather than games consoles. Toys begged you to use your imagination rather than rewarding you for simply pressing a button.

Why not create a vintage nursery or playroom with a sense of nostalgia and innocence? Follow these ideas to take you back in time and get hours of enjoyment watching your children playing with your old favourites.

BOOKS

We should all read a bedtime story to our little ones, but why not consider a vintage story book? In 1940 Ladybird published their first series for children, which included stories such as *Bunnikin's Picnic Party*. These were simple stories told in verse with colourful pictures. Children loved them for their simplicity; parents loved them for their educational value and low price.

The Key Word Reading Scheme introduced in the 1960s helped children to recognize simple words quickly and the method still works today. Be careful though as some are not now considered politically correct (for example, A is for Armoured vehicle) and women may take offence at the role of 'mother', which isn't what it is today! Vintage fans will love the pictures from the 1950s editions with swing dresses, handbags and pretty teacups.

These classic books, along with Beatrix Potter and A. A. Milne, will remind you of being read to as a child and are still loved today. Collect them with the dust covers on for added nostalgia!

Ladybird books, 1950s–1970s

STYLING TIP

If your Ladybird book has pages missing don't discard it. Cut the remaining picture pages into bunting triangles. Choose a matching ribbon to fold over the top and stitch or glue into place. Use the bunting to decorate a child's room.

1940S/50S TOYS

Metal toys were popular in the 1950s, often mirroring the grown-up toys that our parents used, such as typewriters and sewing machines. Before this time, children were working more than playing and therefore had fewer toys, often playing with just a few favourites. These would be hand-crafted wooden toys, such as dolls, trains and boats.

In the 1940s, toy factories were given up to the war effort so in the 1950s there was a boom in production. Classic metal toys to fill your playroom with are the spinning top, kaleidoscope and musical instruments, such as a tambourine. Chad Valley made a great selection of these in primary colours with cute kids on.

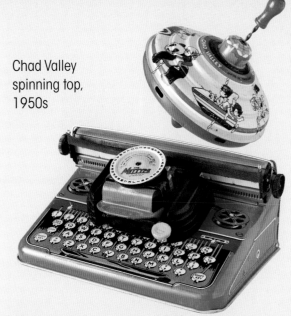

Chad Valley spinning top, 1950s

Mettype Junior typewriter, 1950s

STYLING TIP

Brighten up a toy shelf with vintage metal toys, adding touches of nostalgia as well providing great play. Cluster them together at one end in between piles of vintage books and annuals.

1960S/70S TOYS

In the late 1960s robust plastic toys made by Fisher Price became popular. A favourite is the record player with lullaby records: turn the winder, move the stylus and listen to nursery rhymes. These are simple, mechanical and importantly, still working today.

Fisher Price also produced a telephone, radio and TV – still replicating the grown-up toys just as a decade earlier. Imaginative play was the key focus with the airport, garage and school house. They're not just for older children either: the Happy Apple, chime ball and cot activity centre stimulate early senses and are perfect for a nursery.

Selection of Fisher Price toys, 1960s–1980s

Watch Out!

Fisher Price toys are dated so make sure you are buying an original before you invest as popular versions were reintroduced much later. Ensure the stickers are all intact. Any toy that comes with extra people and accessories is worth buying as sometimes the people alone can cost extra.

DOLLS

Every little girl loves a doll and the vintage ones are the best. In the 1950s, hard plastic dolls made in England by Roddy, Pedigree and Rosebud were the most desired. With their mohair wigs, jointed limbs and blinking eyes, they will really add that vintage look to a nursery.

Dress the dolls up in vintage rompers, sit them in a wooden high chair, wheel them around in an old pram, rock them in a wooden crib – all will add theatre to a little girl's room. For boys, choose a stuffed horse on wheels to help with those first precious steps.

Push-along dog, 1950s

STYLING TIP

Dress your dolls in vintage baby clothes to add extra girliness and a charming look.

Selection of board games, 1950s–1970s

GAMES

Board games from the 1950s onwards are great to play with as a family. Put down the television remote control and compete with old favourites, such as 'Housey Housey' (1950s), 'Cluedo' (1960s), 'Ker Plunk' (1970s) or 'Jaws' (1980s). Apart from being fun they look wonderful stacked up on a playroom shelf. Outdoor toys are also great, with the Fisher Price roller skates, inflatable orange space hoppers and of course the Chopper bike.

Fisher Price roller skates, 1980s

FURNITURE

Vintage home furnishings soften any nursery with their pastel colours and homemade feel, such as chunky knitted cot blankets and character curtains. Store toys in a floral-topped ottoman; perfect for a little girl with its cute flowers, soft styling and plenty of space for all her things.

Children's tub chairs of the 1950s are a perfect size for your little ones and can mirror your adult ones. These come in bright plastic weave or in a natural straw. Old school desks provide a great space for doing their homework or for simply storing their precious retro Lego in. Choose one with the original ink well and matching chair.

In the 1950s painting furniture was popular, in pastel shades such as duck egg. These make great sets for a girl's bedroom especially with a dressing table and fabric-covered stool.

STORAGE

Keep the room tidy by storing pens and chalks in vintage tins. Early sweet tins often came with children's pictures on. Huntley and Palmer's produced iced biscuit tins with Noddy and Muffin the Mule on, Sharp produced toffee tins with an animated Noah's Ark on, even the early Quality Street tins would look great. Old baskets are also ideal for storage and can be carried around your home by your little one.

Watch Out!

These desks came from real schools so check them over before buying for any graffiti that you don't want your little ones to read!

Double school desk and chair, 1960s

Child's tub chair, 1950s

STYLING TIP

Adorn out of reach shelves with vintage ceramics. Characters such as Holly Hobby and Peter Rabbit on vases, bells and bowls will give a nursery a personal feel. These were traditional christening presents that would always be on display.

Sharp & Sons sweet tin, 1960s

GET THE LOOK: Kitty's bedroom, Bedfordshire

The wallpaper in three-year-old Kitty's room is an original 1960s design that was on all four walls when we moved in. Now used as a feature wall it is teamed with white walls and cream painted floorboards. The duck egg and lilac colours are really pretty and not usually the choice for a little girl, with many preferring bright pink. The furniture is 1950s, which was painted by my Great Aunt but could easily be done now. The prints on the wall are vintage pictures of innocent children playing outside, adding a real sense of nostalgia.

GET THE LOOK: Kitty and Herbie's playroom, Bedfordshire

The playroom is a bright orange and yellow room crammed full of retro toys. We have created a unisex room with an original 1960s light and flower curtains. Five-year-old Herbie is becoming a collector like his parents with his great collection of Tonka trucks, robots and books. The old school desks are the perfect place to do homework as well as colouring in. We find grown-ups love this room as much as the kids as, at every turn, something reminds them of their own childhood!

The Study

Working from home is a modern trend, with many of us enjoying the flexibility this brings, especially when managing our own business. With the arrival of the home computer in 1981, internet in the early 1990s and efficient broadband in more recent times, having a study or home office has never been so popular.

In the 1930s father would have sat at his desk in a smaller room or corner of the living room, but this was only in very affluent homes. Unlike today the lady of the house would not have used this space, nor would the children. By the 1980s homes would make a smaller room downstairs into a working space with a desk in. The telephone would be positioned here so families could at last have some privacy after years of sitting in the hallway.

At this time office stationery became colourful with bolder shapes and styles; the in-tray turned from grey to bright red almost overnight and the desk top calculator became the must-have work accessory.

Teak bureau cabinet, 1970s

Must-have Items

DESKS

For a vintage desk your best option is to use a dressing table and remove the mirrors. G Plan's Fresco range in a glossy medium teak comes with two sets of side drawers and a pull-out slimline drawer for stationery. The mirror can then be hung in your bedroom or hallway. Alternatively, use a bureau with a pull-down door to position your laptop on. A more easily found solution is a 1960s cocktail cabinet as this also has a pull-down door front and an inner light. They come with a lock and key for added security as well as a lower cupboard or drawers.

STYLING TIP

Any vintage chair is fine; however, if you are working regularly you should have a modern desk chair as this is best for your posture. This can be re-covered in a hard-wearing vintage fabric, such as tweed. It can be done by a professional re-upholsterer (see Directory at the back of the book) who can advise on material. Welsh tweed chairs are great as they will add a blast of colour to your workspace giving a true retro vibe to your study.

Watch Out!

Cocktail cabinets have an inner light that will need to be tested by an electrician before use.

Filing cabinet, c. 1970s

RECLAIMED STORAGE

Old industrial filing cabinets make fantastic storage in your vintage study. These have often been rescued from old schools, hospitals and factories and come with all the character from decades of use. The slimline, multi-drawer cabinets on thin legs with their original handles and label pouches are great to store all your household paperwork as the drawers are A4 size (US Letter). Desktop drawers make great storage for stationery and are available in metal or wood. For large storage, such as artwork, invest in a 1930s plan chest with thin, wide drawers. These are often oak and are beautiful pieces of furniture in themselves.

RESTORATION TIP

Storage with metal drawers are often painted and covered in marks. This in itself can look great for a vintage feel, but if you want them to be more industrial and polished they can be stripped back to the original metal and given a high shine or painted a new colour. This will take time and effort so be patient and try on a small desk top drawer first.

Work in a well-ventilated area, such as a garage, with safety goggles, gloves and respiratory mask. Empty the cabinet fully and lay out on plastic sheeting. If the handles are removable, take them off and store safely. If they are not, then cover with masking tape. Scrub inside and out thoroughly to remove as much surface rust as possible. Dampen wet/dry fine grit sandpaper, such as a 500 grit, and sand the whole unit gently. This will need to be done many times using finer sandpaper each time until you get down to bare metal. Hose down the unit and wash with sugar soap and warm water. Brush with a stiff brush then rinse and leave to dry. If you want a painted finish, spray a fine layer of primer all over. When totally dry finely spray paint two layers of your chosen colour, leaving it to fully dry between coats. Alternatively, for a high shine, silver finish, after cleaning it with the sugar soap slowly rub in a metal polish using a soft cloth. To finish, replace the handles with originals or new ones.

ANGLEPOISE LAMPS

In the early 1930s, the anglepoise lamp was designed using a newly developed concept of balancing weights using springs and levers. This enabled a light to be angled in any position, which was perfect for both work and study.

The first lamp was made by the British company, Herbert Terry and Sons and designed by George Carwardine, a car designer. First shown at the British Industries Fair in Birmingham in February 1934, this four-spring design was an instant hit. However, it took another year for the design to become less cumbersome with one spring less and now aimed at the domestic market. One version was even used throughout World War II to provide light for the navigator's chart table in Wellington Bombers. In the 1950s the design really took off, with the use of lighter steel and franchising the design out to Europe and America.

It is now considered a true British design classic, appearing on a set of stamps in 2009 alongside the Mini car and Spitfire plane. Many retailers have been influenced by the style, but there is truly only one anglepoise lamp, and this spring patent has been going strong for over 80 years and can be bought new today.

STYLING TIP

The stamps celebrating British design classics can still be bought on auction sites. Display them in a frame to hang on your office wall so you can celebrate great design every day. If the stamps are unused don't stick them to the back paper as this will devalue them. Lightly pin them to card using fine sewing pins, folding them behind the card.

Anglepoise 90, 1980s

Watch Out!

Vintage lights up until the 1980s will probably not have modern wiring. Where possible you should buy a Portable Appliance Tested (PAT) light, but if in doubt get your retro lights checked by a qualified electrician.

DESK CLOCKS

Every desk needs a clock to remind you it's time for lunch! The Big Ben clock by Westclox makes a great addition to your workspace. Westclox started its life as the United Clock Company in the late 1800s in Connecticut, US. After a few bankruptcies they reformed as the Western Clock Manufacturing Company and designed the Big Ben alarm clock movement. This had an integral bell at the back and was famous for being the first alarm clock, as early as 1910.

They continued to revolutionise alarm clocks, being the first to design the snooze mechanism in 1959. The 1970s Repeater model made in their factory in Scotland has the classic space-age styling, with its silver tulip base and coloured dial. While traditionally a bedside clock this won't look out of place in your modern vintage study.

Purple Westclox Repeater, 1960s

STYLING TIP

Create a feature mood-board wall full of design images to inspire you while you work. This could be a large magnetic board or a hand-painted blackboard. Cut out images from magazines, print photos – the list is endless. I love this wall belonging to Justin and Adelle as it is colourful, fun and slightly haphazard. The vintage green kitchen clock in the middle adds a touch of practicality and draws your eye centrally, breaking up the images.

DESKTOP STYLE

Dress your desktop with all these must-have accessories. The desk calendar will remind you of the date as well as add a small piece of history. For a more classic look choose a 1930s glass ink well for your fountain pen. Team it up with vintage letter scales, especially useful if you run an internet business that relies on postage!

Crayonne, sold through Habitat in the 1960s, designed great glossy record racks in oranges and reds, which are perfect for filing. Or use a 1950s ball feet magazine rack for your large papers and the small version for your letters.

For a more retro look choose an early desktop calculator. With its large buttons and red LED numbers, doing your accounts will be so cool!

Desk calendars, 1950s–1960s

Desktop calculator, 1970s

Pressed glass inkwell, c. 1930s

Letter weighing scales, 1950s

GET THE LOOK: Heather and Cleveland's home office, Leeds

The orange retro accessories alongside a modern computer remind us that working can be fun! Add the patterned wallpaper with Jazz framed prints and the design classic white chair and they have created a space you'll want to be in!

" HEATHER SAYS:

When you buy vintage furniture, you know that it has an authenticity, a sense that it has been designed with a particular aesthetic at a particular time in history. "

The Garden

Amateur gardening was a popular pastime in the 1930s, with rows of neat flower beds in the front and back gardens of the newly built suburbs. These quickly turned into allotment-style gardens in the 1940s as the government asked us all to 'Dig for Victory'. Before this time much food came from overseas, but this stopped during World War II so the need to 'grow your own' was more important than ever. This was done by the women, who also kept livestock, swapping eggs for vegetables with their neighbours and adding to the wartime community spirit.

The 1950s saw a return to the 1930s garden, with the men of the house taking over, growing prize dahlias as well as marrows. The lady looked after the house, but outside was clearly his domain along with his garden shed and greenhouse. Children enjoyed being outside too, spending most of their time here after school.

With the introduction of garden centres in the 1960s, for the first time families could buy anything from ponds to tools, making the process of gardening much easier. Gardens could now be built in a weekend, complete with fully grown shrubs, pastel-coloured crazy paving and a cheeky gnome to finish the look. The love affair with the great outdoors and making sure you had the best garden on the street has continued to the modern day. However, we now are looking to the past for inspiration, sourcing materials, such as old railway sleepers as well as using vintage storage as planters.

Must-have Items

FURNITURE

Deck chairs became popular in the 1920s as they were used on holidays rather than at home. Rows of wooden-framed chairs with brightly-striped canvas were positioned on the decks of ocean liners so the affluent traveller could look out to sea. They were also used at the seaside on promenades and piers; hiring out a deckchair by the hour became the perfect pastime in an age of enjoying life and spending time with loved ones.

With the rise of camping trips in the late 1950s, families sat on folding metal chairs, still with striped canvas. These were more portable and could easily be thrown in the back of the car. By the 1970s the fabric had changed to large flowers and there were matching sun loungers and footstools.

Another favourite chair in the 1950s was the woven tub or bucket chair on metal legs. These would have been indoor chairs taken outside on a sunny day, almost like conservatory furniture. All make great furniture now and help to give your garden that vintage feel.

Watch Out!
Don't leave vintage chairs out in the rain or over winter as they will fade or worse still, rot.

Deckchair, 1940s

Bucket chair, 1950s

Camping chair, 1960s

PICNICWARE

In days gone by when the sun came out families packed up the car or the baskets or the bikes and went for a picnic. Picnics in the 1940s and early 1950s were eaten from china plates with proper cutlery. Brexton and Sirram made perfect sets in small, hard suitcases with pretty china, held in place by leather straps. They would always contain a flask for your obligatory cup of tea, drunk from a teacup. A blanket was thrown down, with the adults sitting on folding chairs and the children on the ground. The Morris 8 car had leather seats that could be removed for the adults to sit on. The youngsters ran off to pick wild flowers, which were placed in a vase in the middle of the rug. Sandwiches were wrapped up in greaseproof paper and ham eaten straight from the tin as plastic storage had not yet become popular.

The ladies wore summer dresses, the kids flew kites and the men watched on, dressed in a suit. Even on beach trips the men would be quite smart, with their trousers rolled up to paddle in the sea. Things really changed in the late 1950s with the increased popularity of plastic. As families started to enjoy camping trips rather than staying in traditional boarding houses, they fell in love with the durable, fun-coloured melamine made by Melaware and Gaydon Melmex.

The TV dinner concept took over the camping/picnic world in the early 1970s with stacked trays, plastic cutlery and a space for drinks. The Pac-A-Pic, with layers of orange and white trays, is by far the funkiest way to eat outside.

Watch Out!

Many of the cased sets are sold without their original contents and this should be reflected in the price. A Brexton set would have had its own branded cups and plates, and even the cutlery was theirs. It's rare for the flasks to be original as these would have rusted over time so if you find these intact the set is more valuable.

Brexton picnic set, 1950s

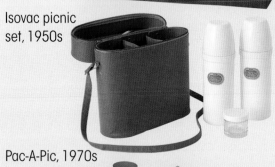

Isovac picnic set, 1950s

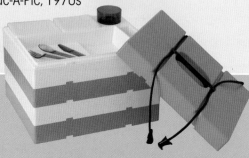

Pac-A-Pic, 1970s

STYLING TIP

Even in small spaces you can follow the 1940s Dig for Victory campaign. Grow vegetables and fruit in reclaimed items, such as 1930s enamel kitchen storage instead of terracotta or plastic pots. Large bread bins and flour jars are perfect for simple shrubs and small fruit bushes. A low enamel bath tub is perfect for shallow-rooted lettuce. Drill holes in the base for drainage.

Swap modern watering cans for metal ones or white enamel pitchers; these will look great left out as garden ornaments, adding to the vintage feel.

The Belfast sink was redundant after the launch of the fitted kitchen in the 1950s. Position these outside the back door for easy-to-pick herbs or individual rocket leaves. Add some gravel or broken terracotta to the base to help with drainage.

GET THE LOOK:
Justin and
Adelle's garden,
Todmorden

"JUSTIN SAYS:

The majority of our garden is laid with granite cobbled sets. We've constructed some small raised beds using reclaimed stone. We have a mixture of containers including lots of galvanised metal dolly tubs and buckets, which we like the look of, plus they don't shatter from the frost. We live in a steep-sided valley, so the garden is shady in parts, which means our hosta and fern collections do well. **"**

STYLING TIP
For a larger raised bed use an enamel full-size, free-standing bath. Plant lines of carrots and spinach as well as flowering plants, such as courgettes to add colour.

Further Reading

This is a list of books, magazines and websites I found useful throughout writing this book – for archive photographs, inspiration, as well as historical information. As most are specialist books you will find further information on topics covered in this book.

Books

Arber, Katie *Thirtiestyle: Home Decoration and Furnishing from the 1930s* Middlesex University Press, 2003

Evans, Paul and Doyle, Peter *The 1940s Home* Shire Publications, 2009

Heathcote, David *Sixtiestyle: Home Decoration and Furnishing from the 1960s* Middlesex University Press, 2004

Hoskins, Leslie *Fiftiestyle: Home Decoration and Furnishing from the 1950s* Middlesex University Press, 2004

Jenkins, Steven *Ceramics of the '50s and '60s: a Collector's Guide* Octopus Publishing Group, 2001

Miller, Judith *20th-Century Glass* Dorling Kindersley Ltd, 2004

Miller, Martin *The Complete Guide to 20th Century Antiques* Carlton Books, 2005

Websites

www.pressedintime.com – for information on 1930s pressed glass

www.mbzponton.org – for information on Bakelite

www.ehow.co.uk – for cleaning ideas

Magazines

Homes and Antiques

Vintage *Ideal Homes* from the 1950s to the 1980s

Vintage *Woman's Own* from the 1930s to the 1960s

Vintage *Brides & Setting up Home* from the 1960s to the 1970s

Directory

UK

Shops

Alfie's Antique Market: 13–25 Church Street, Marylebone, London NW8 8DT. Tel: 020 7706 2969

Dregs of Society: 193 Park View, Whitley Bay NE26 3RD. Tel: 0191 2522205

Nannadobie: 16 Gloucester Road, North Laines, Brighton BN1 4AD. Tel: 01273 676778

Pineapple Retro: Lyndhurst Road, Brockenhurst, Hampshire SO42 7RH. Tel: 01590 624429

Snooper's Paradise: 7–8, Kensington Gardens, Brighton BN1 4AL. Tel: 01273 602558

The Old Cinema: 160 Chiswick High Road, London W4 1PR. Tel: 020 8995 4166

Vintage Treasures: 5a The Lawns, Hinckley, Leicestershire LE10 1DY. Tel: 07890 939236

Online

H is for Home: *www.hisforhome.com*

Retro Bazaar: *www.retro-bazaar.co.uk*

The Oxford Tea Party: *www.oxfordteaparty.com*

Your Vintage Life: *www.yourvintagelife.co.uk*

Yay Retro: *www.yayretro.co.uk*

Specialists

1950s location shoot: *www.planet-sputnik.com*

Cushions/re-upholsters: *www.eclecticchair.co.uk*

Ercol restorers: *www.corwell.co.uk/ercol.php*

Framed magazines: *www.vintageinprint.co.uk*

Reconditioned phones and record players: *www.retro-bazaar.co.uk*

Fairs

Art Deco fairs: *www.artdecofairs.co.uk*

Deco fairs: *vwww.decofairs.co.uk*

Discover Vintage:
www.discovervintage.co.uk

Furniture Flea:
www.judysvintagefair.co.uk

Mid-century Modern:
www.modernshows.com

The Vintage Directory:
www.thevintagedirectory.co.uk

The Vintage Home Show:
www.vintagehomeshow.co.uk

Vintage in the shires:
www.norhtamptonvintagefair. blogspot.co.uk

Festivals

Festival of Vintage:
www.festivalofvintage.co.uk

Goodwood Revival:
www.goodwood.co.uk/revival

Rhythm Riot: *www.rhythm riot.com*

Twinwood Festival:
www.Twinwoodevents.com

Vintage Style

Alessi: *www.alessi.co.uk*

Anglepoise: *www.anglepoise.com*

Ercol furniture: *www.ercol.co.uk*

G Plan 1950s reproduction
furniture: *www.gplan.co.uk*

Habitat: *www.habitat.co.uk*

Le Creuset: *www.lecreuset.co.uk*

Little Greene 1950s original and
re-worked wallpapers:
www.littlegreene.com

Lloyd Loom: *www.lloydloom.com*

Sanderson 1950s original and
re-worked wallpapers:
www.Sanderson-uk.com/ 50s-wallpaper.aspx

USA

Shops

Annie Laurie's Antiques: 536
Broadway; Cape Girardeau, MO.
Tel: 573-339-1301

Empty the Nest: 1121 Cliff Road E,
Burnsville, MN. Tel: 952-808-2933

Junkyard Gypsies: 1022 31W,
Bowling Green, Kentucky.
Tel: 270-781-5865

Las Venus: 163 Ludlow Street, NYC.
Tel: 212-982-0608

Retro@Home: 3811, San Pablo Ave,
Emeryville, CA. Tel: 510-658-6600

Rocket City Retro: 9 Rosa L Jones
Place, Cocoa, Florida.
Tel: 866-951-8709

Salt and Sea: 230 Winslow Way,
Banbridge Island, WA.
Tel: 206-780-1606

Yesterdaze: 5207 North Florida
Avenue, Tampa, Florida.
Tel: 813-231-2020

Websites

Cleveland Art:
www.clevelandart.com

Deco-dence:
www.deco-dence.com

Three Potato Four:
www.threepotatofourshop.com

Festivals

Viva Las Vegas:
www.vivalasvegas.net

Acknowledgments

A huge thank you to Annie and Trevor, Anna and Steve, Sarah B., Carla and Martin, Justin and Adelle, Heather and Cleveland and Sarah G., for giving your time and letting us feature your fabulous homes.

Thank you to Glynis and Becky from Retro Bazaar, David and Janne Bishop, Keeley from Discover Vintage, Justin and Adelle from H is for Home, Nicky from Vintage in Print, Becky from Retro from Scratch and Claire Turner for the loan of your vintage treasures.

Thank you to Lin Clements and all at David & Charles, Simon Whitmore for the beautiful photography, Jeremy Phillips for the photos of Justin and Adelle's home and Sarah Gorlov for the amazing styling on the Styling Tips.

Thank you to Paloma Faith for taking the time out of your busy schedule to write the foreword.

A personal thank you to Kim for your grammatical support and to my family, especially Mum and Aunty Christine for sharing your memories, which inspire me and my writing.

And finally, to Adam, Herbie and Kitty – for your patience, support, dinners and love, without which this book wouldn't be possible. x

Index

About the Author

Kate Beavis, alongside her husband, Adam, is the co-director of Your Vintage Life, the successful online emporium selling fashion, furniture and homewares. Established in 2010 after 20 years in marketing and retail design, they sell internationally as well as to the BBC, National Theatre, Retail Trust, Cath Kidston and even G Plan. Awarded Website of the Month in Period Living magazine, the company has enjoyed regular press including *Vogue*, *Time Out*, *Homes & Antiques* and *Homes & Gardens*. Kate is an experienced writer, contributing regularly to a range of blogs and magazines and is the editor of her county's online vintage guide. She lives with her husband and two children in Bedfordshire, UK.

A DAVID & CHARLES BOOK
© F&W Media International, Ltd 2013

David & Charles is an imprint of F&W Media International, Ltd
Brunel House, Forde Close, Newton Abbot, TQ12 4PU, UK

F&W Media International, Ltd is a subsidiary of F+W Media, Inc
10151 Carver Road, Suite #200, Blue Ash, OH 45242, USA

Text © Kate Beavis 2013
Layout and Photography © F&W Media International, Ltd 2013, except those listed below

First published in the UK and USA in 2013

Kate Beavis has asserted her right to be identified as author of this work in accordance with the Copyright, Designs and Patents Act, 1988.

All rights reserved. No part of this publication may be reproduced in any form or by any means, electronic or mechanical, by photocopying, recording or otherwise, without prior permission in writing from the publisher.

Names of manufacturers and product ranges are provided for the information of readers, with no intention to infringe copyright or trademarks.

A catalogue record for this book is available from the British Library.

ISBN-13: 978-1-4463-0344-3 hardback
ISBN-10: 1-4463-0344-6 hardback

ISBN-13: 978-1-4463-0345-0 paperback
ISBN-10: 1-4463-0345-4 paperback

Printed in China by RR Donnelley for:
F&W Media International, Ltd
Brunel House, Forde Close, Newton Abbot, TQ12 4PU, UK

10 9 8 7 6 5 4 3 2 1

Desk Editor: Hannah Kelly
Project Editor: Lin Clements
Proofreader: Beth Dymond
Design Manager: Sarah Clark
Photographer: Simon Whitmore
Stylist: Sarah Gorlov
Senior Production Controller: Kelly Smith

F+W Media publishes high quality books on a wide range of subjects.
For more great book ideas visit: www.stitchcraftcreate.co.uk

Picture credits:

Cover image © Rebecca Pierce, p16 © Image by Dducks (http://upload.wikimedia.org/wikipedia/commons/thumb/a/a4/Art_Deco_Vogue_shape_designed_by_Eric_Slater_1930.jpg/1280px-Art_Deco_Vogue_shape_designed_by_Eric_Slater_1930.jpg). Retrieved April 24th, 2013, from http://en.wikipedia.org/wiki/File:Art_Deco_Vogue_shape_designed_by_Eric_Slater_1930.jpg. This file is licensed under the Creative Commons Attribution-Share Alike 3.0 Unported license (http://creativecommons.org/licenses/by-sa/3.0/deed.en). Permission is granted to copy, distribute and/or modify this document under the terms of the GNU Free Documentation License, Version 1.2 or any later version published by the Free Software Foundation (http://en.wikipedia.org/wiki/GNU_Free_Documentation_License); with no Invariant Sections, no Front-Cover Texts, and no Back-Cover Texts. A copy of the license is included in the section entitled GNU Free Documentation License. p66, top © marvellousfurniture.co.uk, p155, bottom left and right © iStockphoto

CLAIM YOUR FREE CRAFT EBOOK FROM STITCH CRAFT CREATE!

Download a fabulous FREE eBook from our handpicked selection at:
www.stitchcraftcreate.co.uk/ideas

THEN VISIT OUR BOOKSTORE TO BUY MORE GREAT BOOKS LIKE THESE...

THE COMPLETE VINTAGE WEDDING GUIDE
By Lucy Morris
ISBN-13: 978-1-4463-0357-3
A practical yet beautiful guide to vintage weddings. Written by one of the industry's leading vintage hire specialists, this book is a combination of lavish, yet inspirational photos, and practical how-to information to assist you in planning a stylish and individual vintage wedding.

TREAT YOURSELF NATURAL
By Sof McVeigh
ISBN-13: 978-1-4463-0318-4
A source book for mind, body and soul, overflowing with ideas from the pretty to the practical, along with Sof's easy-to-follow instructions advice. Many of the projects use the gardener's bounty throughout the seasons to create herbal remedies for skin ailments and cosmetic treasures such as lip balms and bath bombs.

101 WAYS TO STITCH CRAFT CREATE VINTAGE
Various
ISBN-13: 978-1-4463-0373-3
Be inspired to get crafting with this collection of 101 simple craft projects spanning every subject area of a vintage lifestyle, from food and drink and house and home, to clothing, jewellery, and special gifts for every occasion. There is a quick and easy-to-make craft project for everyone who loves vintage.

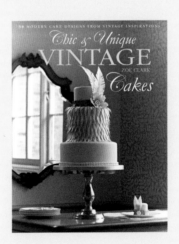

CHIC & UNIQUE VINTAGE CAKES
Zoe Clarke
ISBN-13: 978-1-4463-0284-2
From elegant tiered lace and floral cakes to amazing vintage-inspired novelty cakes, 10 incredible cake designs accompanied by two smaller designs for vintage-inspired cupcakes, cookies, fondant fancies and more. Includes simple step by step instructions for essential cake decorating techniques.

www.stitchcraftcreate.co.uk/books

All details correct at time of printing.